Coping WITH Failure

Shari Cohen

THE ROSEN PUBLISHING GROUP, INC./NEW YORK

Published in 1988 by The Rosen Publishing Group, Inc.
29 East 21st Street, New York, NY 10010

Copyright 1988 by Shari Cohen

First Edition

Library of Congress Cataloging-in-Publication Data

Cohen, Shari.
    Coping with failure/Shari Cohen.—1st ed.
        p.   cm.
    Bibliography: p.
    Includes index.
    ISBN 0-8239-0822-4
    1. Failure (Psychology)   2. Success.   3. Fear of failure.
I. Title.
BF575.F14C64   1988
158'.1—dc19   88-18440
                                                                          CIP
                                                                           AC

Manufactured in the United States of America

ABOUT THE AUTHOR ◇

Shari Cohen is a native of Minneapolis, Minnesota. She attended the University of Minnesota, where she majored in English and Journalism. In 1972 she moved to Los Angeles and began working for the federal government in the space program.

During that time she began working part time as a free-lance writer, contributing human interest stories to newspapers and magazines nationwide.

In 1980 Shari Cohen began writing books for children and young adults. She is the author of the children's books *Macaroni and Fleas* and the sequel, *Blue Noodles on Rye*, and *My Cantor, My Friend*. She also wrote *Coping with Being Adopted* for the young-adult coping series of the Rosen Publishing Group. Her most recent project is a series of novels for handicapped young adults.

She now lives in Woodland Hills, California, with her husband, Paul, and three children, twins Adam and Stephanie, and Barry.

Contents

#1

It may be a comfort to know
that you are not alone
in fearing that of the unknown
in backing down
in avoiding change
in feeling timid
and sometimes strange.
But is also a comfort to know
that you have the power
to stand alone
to challenge
to take risks
and to ask "why?"
to move forward
ahead of the next guy
to walk tall
to smile and confess
that in your heart
as you ALWAYS knew
you are a #1 success!

Shari Cohen

Introduction

Meaningful relationships, good grades, exciting job opportunities are not impossible goals. They can be yours if you want them. At no other time in life will you have as many important decisions to make as you do right now. It is only natural, then, that you want to work at making those choices the right ones.

But it is also natural, at this time when you are trying to make the right moves, to feel frightened and upset when things go wrong. Trying for something you really want and failing can be shattering to your ego. How easy it is to walk away from the disappointment and lay the blame on someone else. Or to stay in the same familiar pattern of doing things for fear of what might happen again.

It takes great courage to accept responsibility for your own choices. Whether it be in school or in a new job, a challenge will always stand before you in life, waiting to be tackled. It's tough to deal with a challenge, though, when the risks of failure appear so great—when you say to yourself, "If I go after it and fail, I'll look ridiculous... I'll lose everything...others will laugh."

Few of us like to be laughed at or criticized. It implies that we are not doing something right. Throughout this book we will talk about dealing with this kind of criticism. We will also discuss "the need to be perfect" and getting rid of certain words in our vocabulary, such as *can't, won't, shouldn't.*

By reading about the failure and success experiences of others, you will see how you too might take a new course of action in going after what you want. You will learn to explore new pathways and bounce back from personal setbacks.

Perhaps you are one of the many who are so afraid of failing that you would rather pass up an opportunity than risk making a mistake. You know that you really want something, but you will not go for it for fear of the consequences. When exposed, however, these earth-shattering consequencs are only minor setbacks on the way to your future achievement.

Perhaps you will come to realize that failure, in a sense, is really a teacher. It enables you to see results in a first, second, or third attempt and to ask, How can I approach it differently this time? What other course of action can I take to get what I want? Then, if you do fail, at least you can have the pride of knowing that you *will* survive. That you have conquered the *fear of failure.* And what a great feeling it will be to know that you have won the first battle in becoming the person you truly want to be.

Isn't It Awful!

L et's face it, nobody likes to lose. Whether it be try-outs for the school soccer team or a bet on Sunday's Super Bowl, that momentary sting of being on the losing end is felt by many of us. It shouldn't hurt. After all, it's only a temporary setback. There will be other soccer games, other events to bet on, right?

Not so with a vast number of people. It hurts a lot. The experience of failing is often so humiliating, so dev-astating, that some people will never again attempt anything along similar lines. Why? Because they have a *fear of failing*. They fear being laughed at. They fear being exposed, and they are concerned about what others are saying or thinking about them. The thought of losing in front of others is enough to keep them spinning in the same familiar pattern of *not* doing things. They will not break out of this safe and comfortable cycle. Trying something new or competing with others is too much of a challenge, a challenge they feel they might fail to meet.

Perhaps you are one of those people. It is surely noth-ing to be ashamed of. It is far better to acknowledge the feelings than try to hide them, pretending that they don't exist. By admitting to yourself that you could possibly carry with you a *fear of failure*, you can begin to explore the reasons behind it. You can look for ways to conquer that fear and head off in a new direction, trying exciting things that you've always wanted to do but were afraid to for fear of what might happen.

Many people hide their talents and strengths—the very things that make them special—just to blend into the crowd unnoticed. They purposely stay out of the limelight in the shadows where their shyness can remain invisible. How many times can you remember doing such things as:

- Not raising your hand in class for fear of giving the wrong answer and being laughed at.
- Not trying out for a part because you'd have to read for it in front of the director and others.
- Singing softly in the chorus for fear of hitting a wrong note and being heard above the others.
- Not showing up at school on the day you were to deliver your speech.

Alongside the *fear of failing* lies the fear of actually succeeding. For what will happen if you suddenly get something you go after? Your life will change in some way. That change, the moving forward in a new direction, is an unsettling feeling. There will be new people to meet, new roads to take. For some people the thought of succeeding is intimidating. They choose not to go after something, to stay in the backround, rather than risk the challenge. They have conflicting feelings about what might happen if they succeed.

- I might have to leave home and be on my own.
- I may have to travel.
- I will be called on to participate.
- My face will be recognized.
- My name will be known publicly.

Perhaps you suspect that you might be one of those afraid to succeed for one reason or another. See if any of these examples are familiar:

- I hide what I really want because I am not sure what others will say.
- My feelings are hurt easily if someone offers me criticism.
- I often know the solution to a problem but will not offer my advice for fear of possibly being wrong.
- It hurts when other people laugh at me even though I'm trying to be serious.
- I often find myself using sarcasm to hide my real feelings.
- I sometimes make impossible demands on myself.
- I'm afraid to make a commitment.
- I'll try something once, then walk away from it if I fail.
- I am ashamed to make mistakes.
- I am jealous of others who achieve what I want and can't get.

If you have spotted yourself in some or several of those examples, chances are you are having a hard time *coping with failure*. The first step after admitting that is to open your mind to suggestions. These suggestions may be the ability to question or accept what has come your way.

You may seek an alternative route toward your goal and overcome the fear that holds you back. Explore new avenues. Listen to what others are saying, others who are where you want to be. Use what you know as stepping-stones toward achieving success. But how do you begin? you may be asking. What is the first step in getting out of this cycle and onto a different track?

Learn to Trust Your Hunches

You can start by listening to the voice within you, trusting your own feelings and your intuition about certain things. Have you ever been told that there was only one right answer to a question, or only one way of doing something? You may have been told that in *words*, but you didn't *feel* that it was right. You felt that perhaps you would have given a different answer or chosen another plan.

You had a hunch that the person was giving you wrong information. And often the other person *is* wrong. Then you find yourself saying, "I should have done it *my* way. I had a *feeling* about this."

Throughout life we experience things that just *feel* right. Even though we may have had no previous training in a given area, we feel comfortable, confident taking a chance. Maybe you feel comfortable speaking in front of a large group of people. Talking to a person on a one-to-one basis makes you tense and uneasy, but in front of a crowd you feel at home. Many comedians and performers express those very same feelings. They say that they can let loose in front of a large group in an auditorium or even a packed stadium. But ask them to talk to a studio head at a lunch meeting and they sweat about it for days. How many times have you read interviews with actors and recording stars who say, "I always knew I wanted to be a star. When I was a kid, I'd put on shows for anyone who would listen." That inner voice that leads us in a certain direction can make it easier to choose what is right for us. And if we ride with that feeling, we learn to better trust ourselves and our choices.

RON: I see you are applying for the job as a veterinary assistant.
TED: I hope I get it. The interview went well.
RON: But why this job? I always thought you would go into sales.
TED: I've always had a way with animals, ever since I can remember. I find them fascinating. I'm also interested in studying medicine. It seems like the right direction to go.
RON: What if you don't get it?
TED: I've decided that I will look for something along the same lines. It feels like the right choice for me. I'm going to go for it.

An artist does not follow a step-by-step art book explaining in detail how to paint a river scene. He uses his basic knowledge of painting and follows his *instinct* on how his finished picture will look. The fiction writer does not follow a reference book saying what she *should* write to sell her novel. Sure, there are rules and basic formats available to follow. But creative people learn to trust their feelings on what will be successful for them.

A well-known writer who specializes in archeological expeditions would probably not want to spend much time trying to write and sell an illustrated children's book. In all probability he could have written and sold the children's book. It's done all the time. But he knows that his *strength* in writing lies in a totally different direction. He writes about artifacts uncovered from millions of years ago. He may stop and reconsider his notion to do the children's book. He thinks it over and admits that the area is unfamiliar to him. He may waste valuable time on it. He decides to listen to his inner voice and achieve success in another way, a path that is more familiar to him.

Trying Too Hard

For some people, analyzing their own strengths and weaknesses is no easy task. They may try for something that is totally unfamiliar to them, an unreachable goal, but they do not give up trying. They become obsessed with reaching this goal, obsessed with conquering the failure experience, and spend a lifetime trying to change the unsuccessful results.

Kevin's father, Ben, was a welder. He owned a successful business that he had built and was proud of. But for as long as Kevin could remember, his father had been trying to pass the state bar examination. Ben wanted to become an attorney, but he failed the exam year after year. He studied for months at a time, ignoring his family and letting his business slide. Finally, after many years of failing the exam, Ben passed. He obtained his credentials for practicing law. After the initial "high" of succeeding wore off, however, Ben became depressed and unhappy. He admitted that he had no real interest in *being* an attorney. Looking back, he realized that he had become obsessed with passing the exam, something that always seemed to be out of reach. He could not handle the fact that he had failed and set out to prove that he could succeed. Even though Ben succeeded in passing the exam, he lost his welding business and found himself in a profession that he did not really want to be in.

Some people cannot accept the possibility that they may not be cut out for a certain line of work or a certain job. Instead of trying for something else, they repeat the same attempts over and over again, experiencing the same end results. If they were to take a different course of action, a different path, the might be able to use their talents and capabilities to achieve better results. Perhaps you are one who tends to try too hard for something, only to find that you fail repeatedly. Realize that you may have lost sight of what you are actually trying to achieve and are concentrating more on the contest of winning.

"I am only five feet tall, too short for our after-school basketball team. I knew that they were only picking girls for the new season who were over a certain height. But I wanted to prove to myself and to others that I could make it. I tried out anyway, and when I didn't make it I complained to the administration and to the coach. I said that I had been discriminated against because of my height. I kept calling and sending letters. Finally the coach gave in and let me play. It was terrible. I didn't enjoy the game, and the others were angry at me for pushing

my way into the team. I guess I knew all along that
I was not right for basketball. I never had any real
interest in the game. But I couldn't accept the fact
that they didn't choose me. It was a blow to my
ego."

Developing a Positive Attitude

Okay. You admit that you may be one of those who are
afraid to fail. You even make yourself a promise to listen
to your inner feelings when you try for something in a
certain area. But what now? What else can you do to
help yourself learn to accept failure? What about attitude? Developing positive attitudes and opening yourself up to suggestions will enable you to see your choices
more clearly. These attitudes could be directed toward:

- Yourself
- Your family
- People outside your family
- Unfamiliar situations

It is easy for someone else to tell you to keep smiling
and keep your mind open to only positive things. We
may not be so positive about what is happening in our
lives at a certain time. We may even resort to "pretending not to care" to keep people away, to hide our true
feelings. With that defense we feel secure, especially if
we fail at something.

BARRY: I didn't really want to get into that fraternity. The guys are a bunch of losers.
ROSE: I don't care that Martha didn't invite me

	to her party Friday night. I have more important things to do.
JEFF:	I'm glad they didn't give me the job. I didn't want to work this summer anyway.
PAULA:	I've been told that I could be a model. Me? That's a laugh!
JILL:	He's good-looking and popular. Why would he want to ask *me* out?
DAVE:	It's a stupid magazine. I'm glad they didn't accept my article.

If we keep others out and choose pretending not to care as a defense, we cannot reveal the truth about ourselves. Deep down inside Jeff knew that he wanted that summer job. He never would have applied for it and called the owner three times if he didn't want it. But by *pretending* not to care he was trying to convey a feeling of indifference to others. His guard was up, and he found it easier to deny wanting the job than to admit defeat in his attempt to get it.

And Paula? She had always dreamed of becoming a model some day. When she was a child her parents had a habit of laughing at her, of making critical remarks about her looks. Now, as a young adult, Paula is critical of herself and sarcastically downplays any praise or compliments she receives.

"I wanted to learn to play the guitar. I signed up for lessons and went to my first one on a Monday. I couldn't seem to catch on; I kept hitting the wrong notes. I felt like an idiot in front of the teacher. He told me to give myself more time, but I thought I looked ridiculous. I quit and never went back. Now

I find myself ridiculing and making fun of people who play the guitar. I guess I'm jealous, but it comes out in that way."

　　　　　　　　　　　　　　　　　　Matt, 18

"I failed math in junior high. I didn't know how to do the problems, and I always scored low on tests. I'm graduating from high school this year, but I still remember that experience with math. I tell anyone who will listen, 'I hate math.' I guess when I'm eighty I'll still say the same thing and feel the same way."

　　　　　　　　　　　　　　　　　Stephen, 18

"I'm always the one to drop out when I'm with my friends and we are all trying for something. A baby-sitting job was available that would have been per-fect for me. It was after school and close to my home. Two of my friends went to interview, but I decided not to. I felt that I wouldn't get it anyway, so I stayed home. My friend Jenna got it. They asked me why I didn't try for it, and I said I didn't like little kids. I really thought that I'd be the last choice of the three of, us and I didn't want to be the loser."

　　　　　　　　　　　　　　　　　Diedre, 16

Diedre chose to stay in a familiar pattern of not working for fear of not being chosen for the job. She could not cope with the idea of being overlooked. Had she realized it, even though she let her fear dictate, she is *still* in the same position: without a job. Had she tried for it, she would have had a chance. Diedre used sarcasm as her defense in saying that she didn't like little kids. In truth, she had a natural way with children and would have made a great baby-sitter.

Jenna, on the other hand, was the first to call when she heard about the job. Her parents had instilled in her a confidence in always going after what she wanted if she felt it was right. She had never been one to let grass grow under her feet.

Jenna really did not like children as much as Diedre did. She did not have the patience. And she lived quite a distance from the job. But she had been saving to buy a home computer, and she saw this as an opportunity to get closer to her goal. Had she not gotten this job, she would have kept searching for another. To Jenna, failing is just a minor inconvenience, a temporary setback on her path to success.

Jenna's courage is to be admired. Unfortunately, not all of us can be so confident and determined. It is because we sometimes do not *allow* ourselves to fail, even though failure is a natural and necessary part of the learning process. Sometimes the unsuccessful experience works out for the better, leads us in a new direction.

Jane Pauley has been a co-host on NBC's "Today Show" for eleven years. She explained in an interview that her failed ambition to be a high school cheerleader helped her land a job in television. "At the age of fourteen," she says, "I felt my life was over. I ended up joining the speech team instead, and within a year I became real good. I can't imagine a better preparation for what I do today."*

*Daily News, Los Angeles, California, 9/18/87.

Accepting Blame vs. Making Excuses

Sometimes it is easiest to place the blame for failure on someone else or some other circumstance. Why take responsibility for an unsuccessful effort? How often have you found yourself creating an excuse for why you didn't get something you went after? Do these sound familiar to you?

I don't have my homework because:
- My dog ate it.
- My kid brother spilled cereal on it.
- I lost it on the way to school.

I was fired from the job because:
- The boss didn't like me.
- I wasn't smart enough.
- I live too far from the office.

I won't ask her out because:
- I'm too short for her.
- She'll turn me down.
- She likes Dave better.

Many times the problem is not with the way others view us, but the way we view ourselves. Our confidence level and self-esteem are operating on a low level. We think of ourselves as losing and then we are not surprised when we do. Try catching yourself next time you find yourself creating an excuse. Stop for a moment and take full responsibility for the action or outcome. Turn the situation around and make it work for you instead of against you.

I *really* don't have my homework because:
- I was too tired last night to do it.

- I didn't understand it.
- I was going to try to finish it in class.

I was *really* fired from the job because:

- I lacked enthusiasm.
- I didn't produce.
- I had problems with absenteeism.

I *really* won't ask her out because:

- I'm afraid to approach her.
- I won't know what to talk about.
- I'm afraid others will know if she turns me down.

Next time you catch yourself making an excuse or pretending not to care to mask your true feelings, try to recognize the action. Try to be honest with yourself and accept the results of your own choices.

If you go for something that you really want and get it, you will probably be the first person to announce your achievement. You will in all likelihood be the first person to accept credit for the success. The same holds true for the times you don't make it. Of course you don't have to announce to the world that you didn't succeed, but admit to yourself that you failed. And use that experience as a learning tool for making it better or making it different next time. *Forgive* yourself for failing. Often the only way we can find out what is possible is by finding out what is *not* possible; in other words, by making a mistake.

Realize also that certain things happen over which you have no control. Perhaps you didn't win the race because your competition was in better physical shape. Or the tryouts that you had prepared for were postponed because the director was sick. At times there is nothing you

can do to change the outcome or change the course of
events. Have compassion for yourself during these
times, just as you would a friend.

Trusting your hunches, developing positive attitudes,
and accepting responsibility for your choices are all ways
you can use to cope with failure. They can help you overcome the fear of not making it, and not let that fear ruin
your chances for making future decisions.

By developing and practicing what we have discussed
in this chapter, perhaps you can have a clearer under-
standing of what is right for you. Then you may or may
not decide to give it another try next time. By opening
yourself up to suggestion, you can use whatever happens
as a learning experience for future choices. The exciting
part about it is that there are no boundaries or limitations on those choices. The opportunities are out there
for everyone. They are out there for you.

Let's go on to talk about *families*. How do the Diedres
and the Jennas enter young adulthood with two different
sets of values? What was said or done to each of them as
they were growing up to make one so determined for
success and the other so intimidated by failure? In Chapter 2 we will hear from others about their own childhood
experiences. Perhaps you will see yourself or your family
in theirs.

Different Types of Families

Imitating Attitudes

Parents who love and relate to their children do just that. They love and relate. It is not an artificial act. They really enjoy their kids and try to do the best job in raising them.

Parental love as a rule does not expect total obedience. It does not smother or overprotect. Your parents do not conciously try to stifle or constrict your emotional growth. But many cannot help it. Sometimes, out of a deep love for you, they cannot help being overprotective. This comes out in many ways. You may have been the baby that was kept away from crowds for fear you might catch a cold from a stranger. You may have been the fourth grader who was sent to school with a sweater and heavy jacket in eighty-degree temperatures because your mother thought you might get chilled.

Parents care deeply about their kid's welfare and happiness, but sometimes they go overboard in trying to make sure nothing bad will come your way. Some rationalize that this is for the "good" of their son or daughter, but often it is really an effort to allay their own anxiety. Their fears and concerns are transferred to you over the years.

If your mother is afraid of large dogs, she may automatically go out of her way to avoid them. You may remember her pulling you out of the path of an approaching dog, even though the dog was lovable and friendly. You may remember her jerking your hand away from someone's pet just as you were about to touch it. She may have said, "Never do that, dogs bite," or "You can't trust dogs to be friendly," or "Here comes one, run the other way." After a time you begin to fear large dogs yourself. Not only large dogs, but all furry animals. You can't help the way you feel; it's something you grew up with. Your mother would understand—she feels the same way.

Just as hang-ups about animals, or thunderstorms, or insects are passed on to children, so are other attitudes. These attitudes are about winning. . .losing. . .succeeding. . .failing. Just as there are different types of personalities, so are there different parental values and attitudes about life. There are overachievers, social planners, headline seekers, those who enjoy peace and solitude, braggers,opportunity seekers, overprotectors. The attitudes that your parents hold are programmed into you innocently, maybe through dinnertable conversations or offhand comments about people or events.

Lacking Confidence

Some parents love and care for their kids but have little confidence in them. They doubt their children's ability to make decisions, to succeed. If you are raised in an atmosphere in which your parents have little confidence in you, you begin to doubt your own ability to succeed in life. If your own family does not see you as capable in achieving anything, gradually you begin to question your own ability. You become incapable of meeting life's challenges. You become accustomed to saying, "Maybe I shouldn't do that," "I'd better not try it," "I really can't do it," "I won't put myself through it," "I'm not good enough." You pick up negative feelings about yourself from what is said to you throughout your childhood years and apply them to your present life. And now, as you are reaching adulthood, you worry so much about your ability or inability to succeed that you become dependent on it. For you, life is one big contest: *win* or *lose*.

Breaking the Pattern

Jerry was raised in such a family. His parents were both shy, timid people. They were loners in high school. They both stay clear of any social clubs or activities. They do not volunteer their services; they do not entertain. Jerry's parents are not bad people. They feel comfortable in each other's company and choose to view the world from the sidelines rather than be active participants.

Over the years Jerry has found himself becoming a loner. He often makes excuses for skipping parties. He does not participate in group events. What makes it easy for him is that his parents fully understand his reluctance to reach out to others. They often go so far as helping him make up explanations as to why he cannot attend a school function or social event. But something in Jerry's life has changed. He is graduating from high school this spring. He has just learned that he is being considered to join a popular fraternity on campus. Jerry is overjoyed. He is excited about the prospect of being in the company of some of the best-liked guys at the university; a few of his close friends are also being considered as pledges to the fraternity. It will mean living on his own. It will mean opportunities to meet new girls and attend campus parties. But there is a catch. Jerry has learned that he will have to convince the brothers that he is the right choice for them. This will mean attending functions, introducing himself to strangers, selling himself to others, making himself known.

It was a painful decision. Jerry struggled with thoughts of giving up, of not trying out for any clubs or organizations. He knew his parents would understand, but he had mixed feelings. A part of him was breaking loose, the part that wanted to socialize, to date, to become an independent person. His father had doubts that he would be chosen. He himself had not attended college and had his own views on fraternities and campus life:

- Don't be disappointed if they go for someone else.
- Not everyone is fraternity material.
- You may not have what it takes.
- Live at home. It will be more convenient for you.
- You don't need them to be happy.

As it turned out, Jerry was not selected to pledge that fraternity. He was disappointed, but his disappointment was mixed with anger—anger toward himself and his parents. He did what he could in attending lunches and meeting new people. But when he was passed over he felt that his parents were secretly relieved. They said they felt bad, but Jerry felt they were happy that he would be living at home. Their words held no enthusiasm or encouragement.

Determined to succeed in his own eyes, to be a part of this fraternity life that he found exciting, Jerry searched out another group on campus. He visted their house, he met with the members. He did not give up until each member was familiar with his name and his face. A rapport developed between Jerry and this club. He was asked to join and he accepted without hesitation. He was proud of his accomplishment, and most of all proud of himself for breaking out of the pattern that he had become accustomed to.

Being Overprotected

In preparation for writing this chapter, the author made a survey of young adults fourteen to eighteen years old. Questions about family life were asked. Contributors were asked to write about how their views reflect those of their parents. A question that generated a particularly emotional response was this one: Do you feel that your parents were overprotective of you as a child? If so, how has that affected or influenced the way you act now, your feelings toward life as a young adult. The following were some of the answers.

"I live with my father. My father is the one who was overprotective of me. He still is. He drives me crazy because of some of the things he does. Like, he does not want me to go out on Friday or Saturday nights with my boyfriend, Matt. He is afraid that we will have a car accident or something bad will happen. When I go out with my friend Melissa, even just shopping at the mall, he has to know exactly where I am going and what time I will be home. I think he imagines that I will die if I am out of his sight. Even for a minute. He is always afraid. But this has made me angry. It has worked in the opposite way. I can't wait to get out of my house. I lie to my father. I always lie just to get out."

Cilla, 15

"My parents treat me like one of their friends. They respect me and ask my opinion on family decisions. They never try to run my life or threaten me into doing something. I appreciate them. I will treat my own kids the same way—with love and a whole lot of respect."

Kirk, 18

"My parents say that I am a failure. They used to tell me this back when I was in the third grade and having trouble with the other kids and the teacher. Last year I dropped out of school. I was sixteen. I got in with a bad group of guys. I did drugs for six months, but I am off them now. I am totally clean. I live with my grandparents. They are good people. I sometime feel that I am a failure because I have been told that by teachers and my parents. My grandparents watch out for me like I was two years old. But I don't mind it. It feels good to know they care."

Allan, 17

"My mother is after me because I smoke. At first I hid it from her. I smoked out the bathroom window. But she found out and she was mad. We didn't speak for almost two weeks. Then I started smoking in the house. Not in front of her, but in my room. She opens my door without knocking and screams at me. She cries sometimes. She says that smoking is dirty and I am trying to make myself sick because I smoke. I like smoking. I still plan to do it. She has made me have a certain attitude about smoking and about other things. I plan to let my own kids choose for themselves what they want to do. I won't try to rule them and take away their choices."

Dan, 16

"My parents were definitely not overprotective of me. They always thought I was mature and grown up for my age. I had my first job at eleven helping out at my uncle's bakery in Milwaukee. I started baby-sitting for my neighbor's kids when I was thirteen. My parents have always been proud of me. I am proud of me too."

Teri, 15

"I really love my parents, but I am angry with them. They both treat me like a criminal. They are suspicious of everything I do. They accuse me of stealing things. I only stole one thing in my life...a sweater when I was twelve. They act like I am doing it everyday. They have always tried to protect me and watch over everything I do. It has made me mad."

Rosa, 14

"There are eight people in my family. I have three brothers and two sisters. I am the youngest. My whole family treats me like a baby. They still even call me 'The baby'. My older sister picks out my clothes. My older brother baby-sits me when my parents go out. I wish they would let me be free and treat me like a *real* person.

Mindy, 13

"I live with my aunt and my cousins. I am from Mexico. My family is very close. My aunt watches over her mother, who lives with us too. I worry about my aunt and grandmother, and they worry about me. That's what families are for."

Carlos, 15

Teens Helping Teens

Think about what you have just read. If you were a school counselor or a best friend to any of these persons, what would you ask or say to them that might help them deal with their problems. Their answers were given to a group of high school students, who responded as follows:

TO CILIA: "Your father is raising you as a single
             parent. Is he lonely? Is he unsure of

how you feel about him? Maybe he is trying too hard to be both mother and father to you."

"Lying will make it worse. He will never trust you if he finds out."

"Have you ever been out late with your boyfriend and made your father worry?"

"Your father is afraid because he cares. If he did not care about you he would not ask what time you will be home. My father never asks. I was not home for two days and he never asked where I was. Be grateful that he worries."

TO ROSA: "You did steal something once. That is why your parents do not trust you."

"When you were caught, were your parents called and brought into it? Maybe they were ashamed and embarrassed."

"I understand how you feel, but I understand your parents too. Stealing is bad news. Do not do it again, because you are older now and you will be a criminal."

"Try to talk to your parents about your anger and your feelings."

TO DAN: "You really are ruining your health by smoking. Try to quit."

"Maybe someone close to your mother has died from cancer."

"Talk to your mother about coming

into your room without knocking.
That is the real problem, I think. You
do not have any privacy. Maybe you
are smoking to make her mad because
she does not give you privacy."

TO ALLAN: "Hang tough. You are lucky to have
your grandparents. Stay off drugs and
keep up the good work."

"Do your parents know that you are
hurt by their calling you a failure? Let
them know. Maybe your grandparents could tell them if you can't."

"Go back and finish school. It is important that you do. If you want to
find a decent job you have to go back
and graduate. Go to college if your
grandparents can help you."

TO KIRK: "It's okay that your parents respect
you. But I don't think they should
treat you like their friend. You are
their son."

"I feel the same way about my dad.
We are good pals. He takes me on
trips. He takes me fishing and buys
me things that I want. Things that
I don't really need but that I just
want."

"I live with my uncle. He is my
friend. I will treat my kids like he
treats me. We get along great. We
are both lucky to live in homes that
have people treating us like people."

DIFFERENT TYPES OF FAMILIES ◇ 25

TO MINDY: "Tell your sister you want to pick your own clothes. She can take you shopping, but you should be able to decide what you want to wear. If it's not *too* crazy, that is."

"We have ten in our family. I am somewhere in the middle. I am also a twin. Sometimes I feel lost, like if I walked out nobody would notice. Your older brothers and sisters will always treat you like the baby, because to them, you are. You will always be the youngest. There is nothing you can do to change how you were born. Learn to live with it."

"Be happy that you have a large family. I do not have any brothers or sisters. A big family sounds like fun. Imagine that you are me and there is no one who will help choose your clothes except your mother. Let's trade families."

"Have a family meeting and tell your parents and brothers and sisters how you *feel*. Tell them not to call you baby, that you don't like it."

Getting the Message Through

Another question in the survey was this: If you were able to change one thing about your parents and their re-

lationship with you, what would it be (in one sentence)?
The following were some of the answers:

- I would want them to pay more attention to how I feel.
- To have them stop yelling at me.
- Nothing—I wouldn't want to change anything.
- To accept me for who I am and not compare me to my older sister.
- To listen to what I have to say.
- Give me more responsibility.
- Show more emotion and tell me she loves me.
- To accept my friends.
- Not to be disappointed when I bring home a bad grade.
- I wish my parents would give me privacy and not ask me a million questions about my life.
- Not to slap me around when my dad gets mad.
- I wish I could tell them my true feelings.
- Let me choose my own clothes and my own friends.
- To quit telling me what to do now that I am eighteen.

What do most of those statements have in common?
They are saying: "I need to be me." "See me as an adult."
"I am a person too." "Hear me." "Listen to what I have to say." "I have sensible views."

Loving families provide a warm, secure emotional atmosphere, which is important to a lifetime of emotional security. These families do not have to comprise one mother, one father, a sister, a brother, and a cute dog to be considered emotionally sound and secure. Many of you may be living with just one parent, or a grandparent, or an aunt. It is the relationship between you and the person who is raising you that is important. A bond connects you. It enables you to share values and goals and to have a commitment to one another. And conflicting values and attitudes are common in these relationships, especially during adolescent years. Take a look around you. Other families are experiencing turmoil, heated arguments, and debates. Yours is not the only one. Your complaints of "Accept my friends," "Listen to me," "Give me more responsibility" are heard in homes all around you. They are not unnatural requests. They are pleas for greater independence. You are saying "Look at me, don't give me unrealistic curfews, don't restrict me from seeing my friends, don't shut me out of family decisions."

Okay, the words are out. But sometimes words alone are not enough. Sometimes you need *action* alongside the words. You have to *show* that you are ready to go it alone, to think and choose independently, to begin to take charge of your own life.

What are some possible ways in which you might be able to show your parents that you should indeed be given more responsibility?

- Don't abuse the telephone, staying on for hours so that no one else can use it.
- Call if you are out and going to be late.
- Leave a note with the name and number of whom you are with if your parents are not home when you leave.
- Do not lie about where you are going or whom you are going with.

- Do not throw a party if your parents are out of town.
- Respect your parents' wishes.
- Help out around the house.

Actions speak louder than words. By repeating acts of maturity in your daily household routine, you may begin to change your parents' attitude toward you. They will learn to trust you and respect your desire for independence.

Let's try another. A common complaint is, "You don't accept my friends." What you are saying is, "I feel you are rejecting me when you reject the people I choose to be around." "You don't take time to know the people I like." "You have no interest in me because you have no interest in whom I go out with." "You have not given my friend a fair chance by not meeting her or getting to know her." This is how you feel and what you mean. Now what could you *do* to change the situation for the better?

- Invite your friend over for lunch on a weekend to meet your parents.
- Arrange for a short meeting between your friend's mother and yours.
- Tell your family about your friend's interests and hobbies.
- Do not be secretive about where you and your friend are going, causing your parents to worry.

If you have some of these complaints and are troubled by lack of communication, try showing your family how you feel through action. When you feel as if they are treating you like your five-year-old brother, take action. Show responsibility over and over again to prove them wrong. At first they may just do a quick doubletake or give a curious glance in your direction. But once they have noticed, they will respond.

Freedom of Choice

As we have seen, much of what is said or done within your family circle often grows out of your parents' childhood experiences. If your mother's mother cooked spaghetti for lunch every Sunday, chances are your own mother finds herself doing that too. And guess what you might find yourself doing for lunch on Sunday about ten years from now? If your father grew up in a household where crying was a sign of weakness, you know why he is angry and impatient with you when you have emotional outbursts. It is a chain that links generation to generation, a pattern of doing or feeling certain things. Try to realize, however, that you do have a choice. You don't have to cook spaghetti on Sunday. You don't even have to eat it if you don't like it. You can examine attitudes that are handed on to you, attitudes of courage, fear, weakness, strength, and weed out the ones that are not suitable for you. Recognize the fears and insecurities for what they are; then let them go. Get rid of negative input that will not be beneficial in the running of your own life.

Suppose your father was born with a bad hip. You inherited the same weakness. He has avoided sports through the years because he has been physically unable to compete with others. You have been hearing about it ever since you can remember. "Sports are a waste of time; there are other things in life more important than sports." You heard it at the dinnertable, you heard it in the car on the way to church. But you feel differently. While it may be a physical impossibility for you to hard kick a ball or to be tackled, you find that you enjoy volleyball. Your strength is in your arms, and you scored well in the past few games you played. Now a new team is being formed and you are asked to join. But you have conflicting feelings. You hesitate to accept because:

- Your sister says you should try out for the swimming team.
- Your father says you will be wasting your time and energy.
- Your family is not enthusiastic.
- Your mother is afraid you will injure your hip.

You feel:

- The exercise would be good for your leg.
- You really enjoy the game.
- You like the guys on the team.

You make a decision. You will let go of your father's attitude and dislike of sports. You will explain to your sister that you have no interest in the swimming team. You will convince your mother that your hip actually feels better when it is exercised. And you will accept the invitation to join the team. Can you see that by breaking out of the tradition of not participating in sports, you have opened up new doors to future opportunities? Not only in sports, but in other areas as well. You are able to weigh the pros and cons and choose what feels right and best for you. You are not stepping on anyone's toes or hurting anyone along the way. You are merely deciding for yourself, standing up for yourself and your desires.

High Expectations

"I've been capable of getting straight A's for many years. My grades have always been the main conversation of my parents when they talk about me to other people. Lately I haven't been getting A's. My classes are more difficult this year, and I have more of them. I feel as if my parents are really disappointed. They are pushing me to bring home the A's. Finally I had to talk to them about it. They were pushing me because they were proud to say to their friends that I was a straight A student. They said it was a reflection on them. I told them that I thought they were being selfish. My grades were something I wanted private, for our own family only. They apologized and felt bad. They didn't realize how I felt. I see that Mom and Dad are just trying to make me do my very best. We *need* to talk to our parents. They will help us, and they want to."

Emilio, 17

Emilio has an open line of communication with his parents. But what if he had not been able to confront his parents with his feelings? Or his parents did not respond? In many families the pressure is constantly on the child to succeed. What the parents don't realize is that overemphasis on grades or achievement can result in a neglect of the child's inner feelings, his or her needs and true capabilities.

Feeling misunderstood in this type of situation, a

teenager may give up altogether and fail deliberately. Or
rebel in some other negative way. How many of you feel
that when you fail at something, or make a mistake, you
have disappointed your parents and their expectations?
You feel that your parents don't love you, that maybe
you are not good enough in their eyes? Trying to be a
super kid to please your parents can lead to a number of
problems. The expectations put on you of always having
to be perfect, of always having to perform lead to:

- Feelings that whatever you do will not be good
  enough.
- Depressing thoughts that you are not pretty
  enough or not handsome enough.
- Feelings of being a total failure if you don't win.
- Feeling pressured into doing things that you know
  are not right for you.
- Thoughts that your parents like your brother or
  sister better than you.

You become angry with yourself for not living up to what
is expected of you. This anger can manifest itself in depression, anxiety, and low self-esteem. If you feel this is
your situation, try to recognize what is happening. Are
you doing something you despise just because you want
to please someone in your family? Are you competing for
goals you know you can't achieve because someone else
expects it of you?

It is important to talk with your parents about your
feelings of being pressured. Call a family meeting and
express yourself. Above all, listen to what they are saying. Perhaps they are unaware that you feel pushed into
doing things you feel incapable of. They may have al-

ternative suggestions or give you the opportunity for other choices that will benefit you and make you happier and more relaxed.

Remember that not all of you are cut out to be super achievers. Not all of you are destined to go to college. You may have other strengths. Perhaps you have artistic or musical talents or are handy with tools. The world is a big place with many available opportunities.

It is important to have support and encouragement behind you and your choices. But you must learn to choose what is right for you. It is easier to be motivated by something that fulfills your inner need for accomplishment, your need for acceptance as you *are*, rather than what you have achieved or what others think you should be.

Your Own Plan

Below are some examples that may help you.

- Decide for yourself who or what you want to be.
- Learn to express your frustrations or disappointments.
- Do not compare your family to another.
- Show your true emotions to your parents. They may not be aware of how you feel.
- Be open to their suggestions. They love you and want the best for you.
- Learn that it is okay to disagree, to voice your opinion with your parents, especially if the subject is *you*.
- Listen to their views without making quick judgments.

- Don't threaten to run off and do it your way.
- Try to keep a sense of humor.

Practicing the Positive

Do you remember Diedre and Jenna from Chapter 1? They both came from loving, supportive families. They both had parents who wanted them to be happy and to succeed. But each family had its own way of saying and doing things. These are some examples of what was said in Diedre's home:

- You're a smart girl. But don't show that you are too smart. You'll scare the boys away.
- Don't make waves.
- Don't count on it, luck doesn't run in our family.
- Why run for class president when vice president is good enough?
- Let us choose for you. You're not old enough to make decisions.
- Don't be too aggressive.
- Don't expect much.
- Don't feel obligated to complete it.
- You don't stand a chance.

These are examples of what was said in Jenna's home:

- If you want it enough, go for it!
- Don't take no for an answer.
- Try it, you may find you like it.
- What have you got to lose?
- Use your own judgment.
- You have nothing to fear but fear itself.

- If you don't go after it, someone else will.
- If you don't succeed, try again.

Can you see some of yourself in these two families? Are you a product of Jenna's or Diedre's home? Most of us are somewhere in between. While we would like to have the values of Jenna, we may lean more toward Diedre, listening to the negative and letting it work for us in a negative way. As we have discussed, there are many kinds of families. There are those that speak in naturally loud voices; there are those that are soft-spoken. There are families that are very neat and those that leave things lying around. How we are raised has a big influence on what we think and what we do at the present time. The negative programming that is passed on to us is the force that makes us afraid to move forward, to march on toward new goals and opportunity. It is hard to break old habits. It is hard to forget what was said. But it can be done.

What if you were to learn that Jenna's family was open for adoption? That you could walk in there and adopt their positive attitudes and values as your own. Their determination to succeed and to seize opportunity could be yours too. Open your mind to the possibility.

Forget what has been said to you in the past. Forget what *others* may think. Start by dropping the *can'ts*, the *don'ts*, the *better nots* that you are familiar with using. Pick up new phrases, such as "I know I can do it." "I have as good a chance as the next person." "I want it and I'm going to give it my best shot." Jenna's positive value system is available to anyone who wants it. Take it from her and let it work for you too.

Develop your own freedom of choice, if only by saying, "You know, I prefer the chocolate cake to the other one." Or, "This semester I plan to take biology rather than the algebra class that my friends are taking." Take small steps at first, but learn to take those steps independently. Make personal choices by and for yourself. By so doing you prepare yourself for the major steps through life, the bigger decisions about careers and relationships. And at the same time you develop new attitudes for your own future family. Watch your self-esteem grow as you learn to listen to and trust yourself.

CHAPTER ◇ 3

Striving for

Acceptance

Following the Crowd

Some time ago in a small Midwestern city lived a fifteen-year-old girl named Lucy. Lucy attended an average junior high school near her home. But this average junior high school just happened to offer a dynamite extracurricular drama class. Lucy wanted more than anything to join the class. She had a secret interest in the theater. She found that besides acting, the backstage production part was exciting and fascinating. The class had even announced that they were looking for production volunteers to help out with show preparation two afternoons a week. But Lucy did not join. Instead she sat, two months later, watching the performance from the audience like everyone else.

Why didn't she join? Because her best friend, whose opinion she valued greatly, considered the drama class ridiculous and a waste of time. The friend made snide remarks about the performers and said that she herself would "die" before she would ever get up and make a fool of herself in front of the whole school. She also said that working for nothing two afternoons a week was a "waste of time."

And so Lucy and her friend watched the performance in the darkened auditorium snickering behind their hands, giggling and criticizing the actors. Lucy was following her friend's feelings but never let on to her own. Acting as if she didn't care, she really wished she were part of the drama group. The productions were successful throughout the year. Then Lucy's friend moved to another city, but still Lucy did not join the drama class. Even though the friend was hundreds of miles away, her attitude asked with Lucy. She chose to stay on the sidelines, looking in.

Today, looking back on that time, Lucy says, "When I think about myself back in junior high and high school, I have regrets that I did not break away from the influence of my friends and participate in the things that really interested *me*. But I remember that I rarely made a move unless I had their approval.

"There are still times when I find myself calling a friend to check on what she will be wearing to a function before I make up my own mind. But on most important decisions that affect me in a personal way, I decide for *me*, I do not rely on someone else's opinion.

"Over the years I have found, and I try to stress this with my own kids, that you can never really fail at 'being yourself.' That you have to do things with the anticipation of meeting some failure. You can't look to someone else to see how you rate as a human being, or use comparisons to measure your own worth. You are a unique individual. Your thoughts, feelings, likes, dislikes cannot be determined by someone else, only by you."

The Importance of Friends

During the adolescent years friends are a critical part of your life. Whether it be one particular person, or a group or clique, these people are a major influence on how you feel about the world. Their attitudes and opinions become even more important than those of your parents. In the company of your friends:

- You care about how you look.
- You share common interests.
- You confide your innermost feelings.
- You discuss current events.
- You let your guard down and act yourself.

A common mistake, however, is letting your friends' opinions influence your own decision-making. When you stop and say, "What will the guys think if I take this class?" or "How will Melanie feel if I see the movie that she hated?" you stop thinking and acting on your own behalf. You find yourself backing off, feeling that *they* might be disappointed if you go ahead with something that you feel is right for you. When *they* becomes more important than *I*, you begin to run into problems.

It is a good, comfortable feeling to be liked and accepted. If your buddies wear jeans and blue shirts to the dance on Friday night, chances are you will too. You want to be *in*; it's a secure feeling. But sometimes this security can work in negative ways. Being too secure can

mean—no challenges, no risks, no growth. The security
that you should be concerned with lies within you, your
internal security. By trusting yourself you learn to
handle anything that comes your way. It becomes easier
to overcome failure and meet new responsibilities.

You've seen news stories on TV where a tornado rips
through a small farming town. The neighborhood is in
ruins. But when the newsman approaches a man who has
lost his home, his workplace, all his material and personal
possessions, he says, "I'll make it. I'm alive and my
family is alive, that's all that matters. We'll start over,
build ourselves up again." This is a man who has internal
strength, a determination to rise above the problem and
make it, drawing from within himself.

If you were the one chosen from a nightclub crowd to
come up on stage and participate in a comedy routine,
how would you feel? Nervous? Embarrassed? With *inner security* you could do it without going to pieces.
Your face might be red, your knees a bit shaky, but you
would be able to handle the situation and others like it.

Using your inner sense of security and being able to
step away from the crowd and act on your own are major
accomplishments. It's tough, but it can be done. The
following dialogue is an example:

SETH: There's a magic contest being put on by
          the school. First prize is $100. I signed
          up to participate.
VICTOR: (laughing) You enter? What do *you* know
          about magic?
SETH: (embarrassed) Not a thing, really. But
          neither do Robert and Jim. They are

putting together a short act. I saw their names on the list.

VICTOR: C'mon, Seth. You'll look like a fool up there. Leave the magic to the magicians.

SETH: I've decided that I'm going to practice and I'm going to give it a shot. I could use the $100.

VICTOR: What if you flub the tricks—in front of the whole school? You'll be laughed off the stage.

SETH: It's a chance I'll have to take. I want to do it and I'm going to do it.

VICTOR: You're sure—

SETH: I'm sure.

Worries

Striving for acceptance or approval is common. Many young adults suffer from something called *compulsive striving*. It means running after something that is always out of reach. These people find it impossible to enjoy what they are doing at the moment. They are so busy worrying about the future that they cannot relax and be themselves. Perhaps you find some of yourself in these examples:

- The test was easy, but what about the one next week?
- I'm happy that I made class treasurer, but I really wanted to be elected president.
- Brett asked me out this weekend, but what if he doesn't ask me out after that?

- I made cheerleading this year, but what if I don't make the tryouts next year?
- The rock concert will be great, but what if they don't play my favorite songs?

Besides worrying about the future, some of you may worry about how others see you or what others are saying about you. You are so busy trying to be what you think others want you to be that you can't enjoy just being yourself. You try too hard to be liked and accepted by everyone. Eventually, however, when you try to be liked by everyone, your life becomes unfulfilled. You worry constantly about what others may be saying even though they may be saying nothing.

For example, Jose's anthropology class was going on a field trip to the mountains. His class was chosen, along with other schools in the community, to attend a weekend retreat. They would be exploring trails, collecting rocks, and examining fossils. Jose was one of a few who signed up to go from his class. He went on the trip because he found the class interesting, but he could not relax and enjoy himself. He had a miserable time. He was in a constant state of worry. These were some of his worries:

- Were his buddies upset that he missed Saturday football practice?
- Would the others laugh because he did not know how to set up his own tent?
- Would he have anyone to eat his meals with or would he have to sit alone?
- Would the teachers think he was stupid if he could not identify the fossils?

- Would the group think he was weird for bringing extra blankets?

Jose's weekend was filled with tension and worry. He could not enjoy himself because he was wondering about the opinion of others.

Do you see some of yourself in Jose? Are you one who cannot enjoy a party because most everyone showed up in jeans and you wore a skirt? Do you refuse an invitation to a get-together because you feel you have nothing to wear? Do you not smile because you wear braces? Do you avoid having your picture taken because you feel your recent haircut is too short?

Try the following exercise. Make a list of the things that really interest you. Then in a column beside each interest or goal, write the *real* reason you don't feel comfortable in pursuing that goal or interest. Examine the list. Does the second column involve the opinion or attitude of someone else? A second party?

Desired Goal or Interest	Reason I Am Not Pursuing It
To call a shy boy in my class that I like.	Afraid that my friends will find out and tease me.
To take a Saturday afternoon cooking class at the Y.	No transportation; Mom can't drive me.
To meet an actor whose son goes to my school.	Son will think I'm dumb for asking.
To learn to speak Spanish.	Nobody is signing up for Spanish class; friends are all taking art.
To learn to swim.	Afraid of how I will look to the younger kids who already can swim.
To learn to operate a computer.	Have trouble catching on; feel that teacher will think I'm slow.

To play in a rock group.	Parents say our family has no musical ability.
To learn to drive a car.	Nervous about taking lessons. Instructor will know I am nervous and I may not pass.
To join our church choir.	Friends think it is not cool, want me to save Sunday morning for skating.
To work on the school newspaper.	Cousin who is a writer thinks I may not have what it takes to write.

When you have completed your own list, eliminate the opinion or attitude of that extra person or persons in column two. Cover every reason that involves what someone else may say or think about your interest or goal. Do your goals now look easier to achieve standing on their own, with no one telling you that they're good or bad? Think about it. Are you not doing what you want because of what someone else thinks? Decide right now that you will not be manipulated by others. Strive for your own success, not for approval.

In his book *The Peak To Peek Principle*,* Robert Schuller talks about striving to arrive at new, meaningful goals. He says that "successful persons survive because they work at it...you must STRIVE to ARRIVE." He sums it up in this six-letter chart:

S–T–R–I–V–E

S — Start Small

T — Think possibilities

* *The Peak To Peek Principle* by Robert Schuller. Doubleday & Co., Garden City, New York, 1980. Reprinted by permission of Doubleday, a division of Bantam, Doubleday, Bell Publishing Group, Inc.

R — Reach a little beyond your grasp
I — Invest all you have in the dream
V — Visualize victory
E — Expect success

As you grow older you will realize that your goal is not popularity—it is a satisfactory end result to your own desires. Remember that it is not possible to please everyone. When you try to please everyone, you end up by pleasing no one.

Throughout your life you will be exposed to new ideas, new situations, and new life-styles. You will develop new hobbies and interests. If you follow the rules so strictly within your group of friends, you begin to stop thinking for yourself. You make decisions based on what they think rather than what is right for you.

"It was a Sunday night. I had a pile of homework that was due the next morning. I waited until the last minute on the weekend and thought I'd stay up late and finish it. My buddy Gene called and wanted me to drop everything and go bowling. He laughed at me when I said I was going to stay and finish my assignments. I felt like a fool. I left the books and went bowling. I got in trouble for my work not being turned in, but I was 'in' with Gene. That was more important to me than a bad grade from my teachers."

Zev, 17

"My parents call me a loner. I don't hang out with anyone special. I see people on a social basis, but I don't have a one-to-one relationship with anyone.

I do things on my own; if I want to go somewhere, I
go. I never ask anyone's opinion."

Mitch, 18

"With some people I really don't care if I'm accepted
or not, but with others I really do. The important
ones are the ones that care about *me*, about what's
on the *inside*. I don't care if I'm acceptd by those
who only see the outside."

Jeannie, 15

"If I get in a fight with my friends, I really feel bad.
They are the most important thing in my life right
now. If one of them is mad at me, it ruins my whole
day. I would lie to anyone, even my parents or my
teacher, to protect my friends."

Victoria, 16

"I still listen to my parents on what is right for me,
not to my friends. We have a close family. Mom and
Dad make the major decisions, and I follow them. I
make decisions on what movies I want to see and
where I want to go shopping, but on most other
things I go to them, and they seem to like that I
trust them so much."

Chris, 14

It may be difficult to step out of the security of your
group and say *black* when they all say *white*, or to say *yes*
when they all say *no*. But by doing this you develop your
capacity for independence and growth. You capitalize on
your own special strengths for making decisions, and you
learn to think for yourself.

Those Who Count

Try thinking about yourself if a positive way. What do you think are your best qualities as a person? Jot them down on a piece of paper.

- I am a thoughtful person.
- I am concerned about others.
- I am a trustworthy person.
- I am a good friend.
- People can count on me.
- I am reliable.

Chances are that the qualities you describe are the very same qualities that your friends admire in you. These friends who are drawn to you want to see you succeed. They may chuckle at what you are about to do or question an interest that you may have. But if they are true friends they are excited if you pass an important exam; thrilled if you are chosen for a part in a play. These are the people who count.

You've heard about friends who desert friends when the going gets tough. Perhaps you have friends who don't come around if you are seriously ill, or cease calling if you have experienced a great failure. These people are only around for the good times; when there are problems they suddenly disappear. These people don't count.

The ones who do count, your true friends, stay with you through success and failure. If Zev's friend Gene were a true friend, he would have understood Zev's decision to stay home and finish his assignments. He laughed at Zev's decision, and Zev immediately changed his mind. Chances are that if Zev had accepted the taunting and still stayed home, Gene would have called again during the week and asked him to go bowling.

Try not to be bothered with the opinions of people with whom you come in contact but who don't count, such as:

- The bully who snickers loudly from the audience when you are onstage speaking into the micro-phone.
- The guy in the back of the class who openly ridicules your explanation of a problem.
- The aunt who laughs at you for playing softball because she feels that the game is only for boys.
- The neighbor who says you are wasting your time trying to lose weight by jogging.
- The person who comments that you will never amount to anything.

Look at yourself through the eyes of those you love. You will no doubt find that they have an excellent opinion of you. Sure, it hurts to be laughed at or criticized for our best efforts. But don't let that keep you from moving forward. Take responsibility for your own ideas, your own desires. Dare to step out of the group and say:

- It sounds like fun, I'm joining.
- It's a tough challenge, but I'm going to give it a shot.
- You may think I'm foolish for participating, but I want to do it and I will.
- You say I might lose. I say I might win, and I'm willing to try.

The I's and the Me's may sound a bit egotistical. But if you don't look out for yourself, who will? Yes, it's true that you may lose. You may fail miserably at something. And yes, they all might laugh. But think about it. You are the one that experienced it. They didn't. And as you know, there are no guarantees that you will pass or win or make it in the future. If you have to have a guarantee that everything will be all right before you take a risk, you will never get ahead. The future is predicted to no one.

Some of you may be saying, Okay, I'll try standing up for myself. I'm willing to give it a try. But WHAT IF something happens?

- WHAT IF I faint on stage in front of everyone?
- WHAT IF I'm the only one in the whole class who fails?
- WHAT IF all of my friends are chosen and I'm not?
- WHAT IF I make a fool of myself on roller skates?
- WHAT IF they find out I can't swim?
- WHAT IF no one asks me to the dance?
- WHAT IF I ask her out and she turns me down?
- WHAT IF I go alone to the party and no one talks to me?
- WHAT IF the bases are loaded and I strike out?
- WHAT IF I lose the tennis match?

Let's talk about WHAT IF for a moment. So you lost the tennis match. What have you really lost? Your money? Your health? Nothing, really. You just did not score as many points hitting a ball over a net as the other person. So what's going to happen? Are they going to announce that you were the loser on the 6 o'clock news? Are they going to put the fact that you lost in lights and broadcast it around the city? Will your teacher stop talking to you? Your friends turn away? Probably not. What really could be the worst that could happen in this situation? The audience might boo your loss. But that would only last a few seconds. Then they'd go about their own business. You'd feel terrible losing to your opponent, for the moment. But then, who really cares about this particular loss? There will be other games, other wins and other losses.

Let's try another example. Let's say you struck out at softball. Maybe the bases were loaded and your team needed to score. You feel awful. But what's really going to happen? Are they going to throw rocks at you from the bleachers? Are you a worse person that you were when you stepped up to bat? Chances are, by the time the other team comes up to bat they will have forgotten that you struck out. There will be a whole team of hitters and strikers. The game will go on.

Examining the Worst

Go back for a moment and read over the list of WHAT IF's. Add some of your own personal worries to the list. Write down the very worst thing that could happen in your WHAT IF situation. What catastrophe would come about if you asked someone out and she said no? If you fainted on stage, would people leave you there and stare down at you? Or would someone help you up and offer you a glass of water?

What should be the outcome if the most popular girl

in school said, "Sorry, I don't think so" when you asked her to a movie on Saturday night? Would you retreat to your room and not come out for a week—or never see the movie because the person you asked declined your invitation? It is hoped that you would ask someone else and go and enjoy the movie.

Allow yourself to feel the disappointment, the pain of the loss, but don't dwell on it. Step over it or around it and move forward. Let go of your hurt and pride and make way for healthier, positive feelings.

The Fear of Happiness

Most of us feel that wanting to be happy is great. But you may be surprised to learn that many people feel otherwise. Most are not aware that they hold this belief, but their actions show it. These people stop themselves just when they are on the verge of any success. They get little pleasure out of ordinary pursuits. Happiness always seems to be out of their reach. They walk around with frowns on their faces, shoulders slumped, eyes cast down. They have the love of their families, health, friends, financial success, but they are always miserable.

Just as Jose worried about what others were thinking instead of enjoying himself, these people always feel a sense of hopelessness. Perhaps you are familiar with:

- The father who is openly disappointed because his healthy baby was born a girl and not a boy.
- The aunt who cannot enjoy the pink dishes as a gift from her family, because her favorite color is yellow.

There is nothing you can do to please these people. No matter how many gifts you give them or how many compliments you deliver, they are unhappy.

This is not what any of us want to become. And so we must realize that no one owes us anything. Being happy, having a good time is our own responsibility.

"I am depressed most of the time. I've been in counseling for four years. My problem is that I try too hard to be happy, and when that happiness is not felt, I go into a depression. I tried drugs and was drinking for about a year. When I was drunk or stoned I felt good. I felt happy, but it didn't last. When I came down off the high, I felt worse.

My friend is always happy and in a good mood. She gets excited over anything. I am jealous of her. I want to be her. My family life has a lot to do with why I am having problems. Dad left us when I was two. Mom had to work two jobs. We didn't have money. Mom sent me to live with my aunt. I stayed there for a little over three years. She hates kids, and I was always in her way. I ran away, but I had to come back because I had no money and could not find a place to stay.

I am trying to work out my life with the help of my counselor. My goal is to stop expecting people and things to make me happy. I have to learn to like myself—to be myself. I want to enjoy life."

Karen, 17

"I have trouble making friends. I'm always the one who has to start talking to someone first. I don't know why, but in all of my schools, even from 1st grade to 6th, I have never been popular. I try to be nice to people, get to know them and be their friend. I don't know what more to do. I feel that I don't fit in with others. Maybe I try too hard. Sometimes I become obsessed with who likes me and who doesn't. I just feel that as hard as I try, I am not as pretty, skinny, fashionably dressed, or acceptable as everyone else. I want to be, but I don't know how."

Jill, 16

Do you find yourself unhappy most of the time? Even if things are good in your life, do you find yourself saying, "What's the use?" Or, "Why bother?" Try to understand that it is not possible to have the love of *everyone* or the admiration of *everyone*. Enjoy the smaller pleasures in life, such as a night out with a good friend. Take joy in lesser accomplishments. Don't put yourself in the position of having to have it all on a grand scale. It's true that you can't expect to pop up happy and cheerful when blow after blow knocks you down. But you have a choice of staying down and giving in or getting up and fighting back. Relight that spark. You gain nothing by dwelling in sadness and misery. Don't waste time brooding and waiting for things to come your way. Do things to improve your situation, even if they seem silly or frivolous.

- Let loose, do something just for the fun of it. Take a walk barefoot on the beach by yourself. Re-examine your thoughts and feelings.
- Renew an old friendship, call a person whom you really like but have been ignoring.

- Treat yourself to something special, such as a new hairdo or a new outfit.
- Do something nice for someone without being told. Send flowers to your grandmother, take a younger brother or sister out for ice cream.

Poor Me

Sometimes it's easy to feel that everything good or everything positive happens to the rich or the beautiful people. You may feel that the great-looking guy in school has it made. He's the one who gets all the breaks. He'll be automatically successful because he drives a new car and his parents have money. Not true. The guy you are envying may be good-looking and have money, but he also may be lazy and lack initiative. His looks and his money will get him nowhere when he has to compete in the real world. There are thousands of others out there who are equally good-looking and have money.

Think for a moment about the European refugees who came to this country during World War II. They fled Germany and other parts of Europe to begin new lives in our country. Many well-to-do people arrived with just a small parcel and the clothes on their backs. They had what was left of their families and a few possessions, nothing more. These people had determination to survive and to make a new life for themselves in a new land. They worked hard, in factories and in mills, sometimes at two and three jobs, just to put food on the table for their families. These people did not have the luxury of sitting back and saying, "Poor me, my country is at war, all I have worked for is gone, my relatives have been killed or are missing." They had major catastrophes to complain about, but they needed to survive. They needed to march on toward new opportunities.

Today these people have built up successful businesses, museums, galleries, law firms, schools. They achieved their successes on their own; they looked inward for guidance, not to others. They ruled themselves instead of being ruled by others. And they gained great personal satisfaction from the results of their efforts.

They went after their opportunities with a plan. Looks, ability, talent, money, all can help a person achieve a certain goal. But drive, desire, and internal strength are the tools needed to complete the job.

After high school and throughout your life you will be meeting and competing with people from all walks of life. Whether it be a decision in your career or a personal relationship, you won't be checking back with "the group" before you speak on your own behalf. When you are interviewed for a position as gymnastics coach, you won't say, "Wait, let me talk it over with my buddies before I give you my answer. *They* will know what's best for me."

Learn to think independently. Allow yourself to break free and to feel according to your *own* personal greatness, not that of your friends or an acquaintance. Don't wait until you are out of high school to begin acting on your own. Give yourself permisson. The time to start is now.

In Chapter 4 we will hear from Sonya, an eighteen-year-old girl who has suffered many personal tragedies and failures She is struggling to overcome her feelings of anger and remorse and is on her way toward a successful career and a new life.

Sonya

Q: Sonya, I'd like to start by asking how old you are.

A: Eighteen.

Q: I've been interviewing a number of teenagers regarding personal failure experiences in their lives. Quite a few of them have been having problems coping with these experiences. I spoke with you previously and wanted to come back for a longer interview because of all that you have been through. You have suffered great personal tragedies and problems; however, you seem to have pulled yourself out on your own. You seem strong, happy, and have a positive outlook on what you want to do with your life from this point on. I'm wondering if it would be possible for you to share some of your experiences, if we could talk openly and freely about your past, your present, and what you have planned for your future?

A: Yeah.

Q: Let's start back when you were twelve or thirteen

years old. Besides the usual school problems, I understand that some major events in your life began to happen around that time.

A: A whole lot. School was a minor problem. I was a very good student. My parents had a very bad marriage. They married too young; they did not get along at all. There was violence ranging from mental to physical. I think my dad hated women. And when I started growing up, or becoming a woman, shall we say—puberty—going through changes—growing breasts—I was not looked upon as a daughter anymore. Suddenly I was a woman, I was a slut. And that's when all the physical, the mental abuse came in. Well, actually some of it started earlier, because I would be forced to watch while my dad beat up my mom or something like that, and it just got progressively worse, to where I got beaten. And I got into drugs.

Q: They made you stay in the same room—or he made you stay in the same room when that was going on?

A: Yeah, I'd be staying in the same room, or I'd be calling out for Mom and it would be—"Here, you want to see your mom?" And her hand would be—her arm would be way up behind her back all the way up to her neck where I could hear it starting to break.

Q: Oh, my—

A: It got to the point where Mom killed him. She couldn't take it. She was afraid to leave because he said he'd kill her and he meant it.

Q: When did this happen?

A: When I was thirteen.

A: When she ended up killing him?

Q: Yes.

Q: What happened after that?

A: She went to jail, and my uncle came and stayed here. My aunt was an alcoholic and my uncle was going through problems because he didn't have a job. Then he got a job and we were being supported off my brothers and my social security checks. And I stayed home from school and ditched and I was into drugs very heavily.

Q: Was this all because of that one incident? Were you into drugs at any time before then?

A: No, I think everything started then. I got to the point where I realized that I was different from all the other kids, you know.

Q: Because of the abuse and the violence that was going on in your family?

A: Yeah, I'd go to other people's houses and I'd think, Hey, they're eating dinner and it looks nice; why doesn't my family do that? I just wanted to escape from it, and so I got into drugs knowing exactly what I was doing.

Q: Did you have anybody that you could talk to—a friend, a confidant, somebody—with all this going on?

A: No, because—well, it's like somebody who is getting ready to commit suicide talking to another person who is extremely competent. What can they tell you that's going to help? They have no idea because they don't understand.

Q: So when all of this was going on, were you heavily into drugs? Or were you just experimenting?

A: No, I was heavily into them. I was into them so heavily that I bought books and read up on everything. I started mixing two and three things together and started selling them. My friend that I had grown up with was real smart. She had a chemistry set, and we'd get together and instead of going to school we'd make drugs and sell them.

Q: How old were you at this time?

A: Fourteen.

Q: Who were you living with? Were you living with your aunt?

A: Yeah, and I was living in the same house.

Q: What were your feelings during this time that you were taking drugs? Did you realize that you were headed for trouble? Or did you just not think about it?

A: I guess at the time I didn't really feel bad. It was just an escape. It was an escape from the nightmares, it was an escape from the fact that I saw the whole thing when it happened. I was standing right there at the door. I mean, it's not like I was sitting around crying somewhere. My brother didn't know—he came home and it was like. . .we said, "Go next door." But

I was home and I saw the whole thing. I wanted to escape.

Q: What about now, today? Do you still think back and remember the feelings that you had back then? Are you over it?

A: I guess only amnesia would really make me forget something like that. Once in a while I'll have a flashback or something and then I'll brush it out of my mind real quick. But I can deal with it now. I had no feelings for the man at the time that he died. I had feelings for something that I wished was there that I never had.

Q: A real father—?

A: Yeah. Somebody to call *Dad*. Yeah, he's a father, but there's a difference between a *father* and a *dad*.

A: You must have felt pretty much alone during that time—and lonely.

A: Yeah.

Q: When did it start to change? As far as getting yourself out of the drug scene and getting back on your feet?

A: It was around when I was fifteen. Early fifteen, very early when I first turned fifteen, and I woke up and I was about 108 pounds and my skin was turning yellow and my cheeks were caved in and my eyes were just totally messed up. I looked at myself and I was high and I said, "In a few more days you are going to die." And I asked myself, "Do you want to die?" And I thought—I'm not that bold, I don't want to die yet.

Q: So you just realized waking up one morning that you had pushed yourself too far—

A: Yeah.

Q: When you decided that you were going to get off drugs, did it happen overnight or did it take a long time to clean yourself out and come back to the world, so to speak?

A: It took a lot to get emotions back. I lost a lot of emotions. At that point it was like—Who cared? As far as drugs, since I had read about it and knew what I was getting into, I knew when to get off a particular drug before I went on to the next one, so that I wouldn't get addicted. And I had no problem with psychological addiction at all because I just wanted to get off and I got off.

Q: Did you notice a change in your appearance as you were getting off the drugs?

A: (laughing) Oh, the weight gain. I mean it wasn't that big, but I started going to the gym, which really helped. It built up my confidence.

Q: So you started feeling better about yourself?

A: Yeah. At first it was physically, because even to this day I still have a lot of problems emotionally in just dealing with people—relationships—a one-to-one basis. You know, anything that is serious, really really serious.

Q: More than with a group of people, you mean?

A: Well, with a group of people I'm the comic. I mean everything is just a joke, because Sonya doesn't take anything seriously. You know, for amusement go to Sonya because she's funny. She'll brighten up your day. Well, no one realizes that my days are not exactly the brightest all the time.

Q: But you don't tell people that? You don't confide in them your true feelings?

A: No, because all I can hear is. . .I mean I don't want anybody to tell me what I want to hear—tell me the truth. But what would I hear besides "Oh, that's a shame," or "Oh, I feel so bad for you." Well, that's nice, but I mean, tell me something that's going to help!

Q: So you don't want to hear sympathy from them, you want to hear some words of encouragement—

A: Yeah, give me good advice or something, but nobody can really sympathize because they don't understand my plight.

Q: Did you ever try to talk to a counselor at the school or somebody professional?

A: When I was about thirteen, fourteen, my mom immediately sent me to a counselor. The first one didn't work out because she thought I was an angel and she thought my mom was crazy. (laughing) I really had her fooled. And then I went to another one who was all right, but I was doing it for my mom. I write a lot now. I write in my diaries and I keep stacks of journals that you wouldn't believe.

Q: About your feelings and about what's going on in your life?

A: Yeah, that's the way I get things out. No matter what, what can a psychologist tell you? Okay, he read his books, that's nice. But he doesn't *know*, he can't really experience the same feelings . . . you know, he wasn't there.

Q: Does it help you to write everything down? When you read it over and express yourself on paper, do you feel better? Keeping your own journal of thoughts—

A: Well, I usually write and the thing is, I don't usually read it over. I write and I let it go and it's gone.

Q: Do you get a feeling of relief after you've written? Is this your own way of expressing your feelings?

A: Yeah, it's pretty much my only way. But it works.

Q: It's a way of coping, a different way of coping, writing your thoughts down rather than talking to someone else about it or getting advice from other people. You are listening to yourself—hearing yourself.

A: I figure that's the best way I can get advice from my situation, because the only one who really knows what I am going through is me.

Q: What about now? Are you a stronger person because of everything that you have gone through?

A: Yes.

Q: You appear to be. You seem to be very determined. At least on the outside.

A: Even on the inside. It's like sometimes I look and I wonder if it's stone in there. Because I'm very very hard when it comes to. . . I mean with little kids and things like that. I'm not going to cut anybody up, but when it comes to feelings, emotions and all that other whoop-de-do, it's like, sometimes I wonder where it is.

Q: If you had to defend yourself against something that had been said about you, would you stand up to the person and tell them your feelings now?

A: Oh yeah. . . but usually there's not that much call, because I have this really strange opinion about what people have to say about me, which is. . . if they are my true friends they are going to come to me and ask; if they are sincere about it, they are going to come to me and ask me. If they are not sincere about it, they are not my friends, and I'm not even going to waste my time trying to defend myself. I mean, I wouldn't stoop to their level and try to defend myself against a vicious lie or something.

Q: So you only concern yourself with the people who count in your life. . . your true friends—

A: Yes.

Q: They were there for you before, they are there for you now—

A: And they would be there for me tomorrow. And anybody else. . . I don't care what anybody has to say. If they are going to think bad of me, they don't care about me. And if they don't care about me, they are not my concern. You know, you can spend your whole life trying to defend yourself against what people have to say. They're always going to have something to say. It's petty. I don't see any reason to involve myself in petty things like that.

Q: With your good friends, the ones who count, do you ever consult them before you go after an opportunity? If there is a job coming up or if there is something that you want, do you turn to these people or would you go ahead and do it on your own and then tell them about it afterwards?

A: Well, I guess it kind of depends on what exactly it is. I mean, for a job or something, I'm sorry but if I want to do it I'm going to do it. If I had two good opportunities and I want an objective opinion...what would *you* do? And I could evaluate it later and see if it suits my purposes. If it doesn't, that's fine, but you know, it's an opinion. I respect people's opinions. They're valuable to me.

Q: What about taking risks? How do you feel about taking risks? Are you intimidated by it or...if you really, really want something, would you just go after it?

A: Oh, yeah.

Q: Even with a personal relationship, let's say with a guy, would you go up to a guy that you didn't know and introduce yourself?

A: I'm not intimidated about that. (laughing) I haven't been turned down yet. I don't have anything to worry about. If I want something or if I like somebody, yeah, I'll go after him. This isn't 1950 where I would have to sit back and wait for the guy to say, "Come here." I mean, you take a risk every day when you drive the freeway. I take a risk because I do 85. (laughing) I risk death, I mean you know, some risks are stupid to hide from.

Q: Some people, when it comes to going up to a guy, they take the risk of saying, "Hi, how are you, my name is so and so"—and if the guy gives them the cold shoulder, a blank or a negative response, they fall apart. It is the end of the world for them. How do you feel when you are met with a negative response to an approach, either in a relationship or in something that you are going after and it turns out completely negative? Do you pick yourself up and say, "That's the way it is," or what are your feelings?

A: Well, to tell you the truth, about relationships, I haven't had that much experience in deep ones except for my current one. I never let myself get involved that heavily. But if I was approaching other people...I think the ones that are really turned down are the ones approaching guys who they *know* are not...I guess you could say in their league... someone who is not on their level. And if that's the case, then they probably should never have approached him anyway becaues it wouldn't work. You should really take your time to look...to examine things...to figure out, Do I really want this or am I doing this just to play with him? Because most of the time you will get rejected if you are doing it to play or if you have a real insecurity complex. You say, "Well hi, my name is Kathi"... you know, maybe they'll say yes, if you carry yourself with confidence, there is not that much rejection.

Q: You sound pretty confident. You sound as if you have it all together. I really admire that, especially after all you have gone through. What about on a smaller scale? Let's say these last few years in high school. Were you overlooked for something like...a school project? How do you cope with the smaller failure experiences?

A: The first time I took the pro-efficiency test, I was so nervous. At that time my dad had spent all of my thirteen years telling me that I was an idiot. I was dumb—I mean, I was pulling straight A's but I was "dumb" and "stupid." I had it in my head that I was stupid, and I failed the test because I was stressed out and thought I was dumb.

Q: When he told you that you were stupid throughout your earlier years, did you believe him? Or did you know inside that you really had it?

A: Well, if somebody told me that I'm stupid now, I'd look at them and say, "Who cares? It's your opinion."

Q: But you were very impressionable back then—

A: Yeah, back at that age, what happens in your early life really does have an effect on you. If you are told that you are stupid, it's a self-fulfilling prophecy. If you are told that you are dumb and your parents tell you that you are stupid, you are an idiot, you are incompetent, most of those people end up with insecurity complexes. I consider myself lucky, because most of those people are totally messed up. If I fail at something I say, "Yup, he was right." But then it's like...No, he wasn't right! Because I'll turn around and I'll do it right this time.

Q: So you are determined to overcome all that was said to you—

A: Yeah, like with math. I want to be a lawyer. I have to learn how to think logically, and math is going to help me. But you know, word problems "kick my natural butt!" (laughing) And you know, I'll sit and think and have memories of getting my butt kicked at twelve o'clock at night when I was twelve years old because I couldn't do a math problem because I was "too dumb."

Q: You were physically abused?

A: Yes. Because I was a "stupid idiot" and I couldn't do my math because I was just a "dummy." And "Dumb kids can't do their math" and "Dumb kids are just going to be *dumb* for the rest of their lives." Well, now I'll say—no, I'm not going to let it happen. I'm going to prove you wrong.

Q: So you want to prove to yourself—even though all of what was said to you is remembered—you want to prove that all the negative was wrong.

A: That's probably most of it. My basic motive for doing anything with my life right now is simply because I'm going to prove a point. I'm going to prove to a *dead man* that I can do something *right!*

Q: Sonya, the book I'm writing will be reaching thousands of young adults across the country. Right now, at this minute, you have a chance to say something personal to them, directly to them. You have a chance to give other teenagers advice or opinions on how they may overcome or cope with a failure experience. Their experiences may be with drugs also, or possibly with failed relationships. Looking back on your own life and drawing from your own experiences, what can you say to them to help them at this time in their lives? To help them get up and move forward and deal with this frustrating time?

A: One basic thing, and this seems to be a problem with a lot of people today...they are going by *other people's* standards. Their goals are everybody else's goals. The only person that you really have to compete with is *yourself*. Because Jo Blow...who cares about Jo Blow's goals? You should be setting your *own* goals within yourself. And you can make your own goals. It's when you begin competing with every Tom, Dick, and Harry in the neigbourhood that the problem comes in. You should set your own goals and as long as *you* are fulfilled and *you* are happy inside, that is the main thing. Do what makes you happy.

Q: *You* are the person who counts.

A: When it boils down to it, it sounds selfish, but you *ARE* the one who counts. In anything, even in a relationship...because without you, I'm sorry, there is no relationship. You have to be happy, and that's all that really counts. You can't fail if you are happy.

Q: So you should try to set your own goals...even if it is

just a step at a time...long-term goals? Short-term goals? What are your feelings?

A: You make your goals. Some people have goals just to move out of the house. That's fine. That's a goal. We have unlimited goals and wants...there are always going to be goals. But if you set a goal for twenty years from now, make sure that you are doing things about it today so that in twenty years you aren't going to sit there and say "I failed, I didn't make it."

Q: So have a plan—

A: You have to have some sort of format and think how you are going to go about it, but just be determined and don't pay attention to what anybody else has to say.

Q: And if you have setbacks or if you fail along the way?

A: In some ways, everybody should *want* to fail because you are learning. If you fail, you have just learned something. I mean, you have just said, "I'm not going to do it this way again"...so if you can't go straight through, go under it...climb over it...go around it. It's like swimming at the beach and the waves keep crashing and pushing you back. If you want to get out there and ride them like a surfer, that smooth ride...you have to get out there first. You have to dive into the waves, take your boogie board and plow right through if you have to.

Q: Even though other people might be saying to you, "The waters are too choppy" or "You might fall off."

A: Oh, I'll tell you, that ride back is a lot smoother than the ride out.

Q: Once you've made it, it is easier.

A: Yes.

Q: Is there anything else? Would you like to make a last comment about drugs? There are many twelve-, thirteen-, fourteen-year-old readers who may be experiencing problems with alcohol or drugs.

A: Actually, I'd like to say just *get off*! But you hear it on TV and most of the kids don't use them because they think it's cool. They use them because they have some sort of problem in their life. And again, the most important person in your life is *yourself*. If you destroy yourself. . .you have *nothing*. So keep yourself strong because you have to get somewhere. Don't let drugs. . .alcohol. . .words. . .anything destroy yourself, because that's all you've got, that's your rock.

Q: Believe in yourself, do for yourself—

A: Yeah. Of course, care for other people along the way. . .but I mean, you know. . .*Number one*. Get yourself settled. At our age we have to be number one, because nobody else is going to get us where we want to go, you know, lead us through life. . .besides *us*. Set your goals and go for it!

Q: Sonya, thank you. You've experienced so much, and I think it has made you a stronger person.

A: Thanks, I hope so.

CHAPTER ◇ 5

Experiencing the Loss

t is easy to give in to failure. Whether you've gone off your diet or merely failed to help a person who came to you for advice, that out is always available. Once you've failed at something, how simple it is to say, "Oh, I can't do that again; it didn't work for me the first time." Or "Don't come to me for advice; I couldn't do much for the last person." You may feel that others will understand, because failing at something means that you did at least try it once.

Don't be fooled. The success stories that you read and hear about don't involve people who try things just once. The excuses—"It was too difficult to attempt again," or "Why should I try?"—fall flat on the ears of those opportunity chasers, the ones who strive for achievement. An example that comes to mind is Mrs. Fields of Chocolate Chip Cookie fame. She is the young wife and mother who decided to market her homemade cookies to the public. She started out baking them at home in her kitchen oven. Knowing that she had a marketable product, she began going to shopping centers and soliciting passersby to taste her cookies. She has described her efforts and her determination to make a go of it on many TV talk shows. She told of running after shoppers with her cookies, offeing free samples to anyone. Gradually people started coming back to her, realizing that she did indeed have a delicious product. Soon there were many paying customers, and now she has stores that are franchised in cities throughout the United States. Mrs. Fields believed in herself and in her product. She had a plan, took action, and over a period of time her plan worked.

What do you think would have happened if Mrs. Fields had given up after a bad month of cookie sales? She was not an overnight success; she had many frustrations and many reasons to quit if she wanted. Had she given in, people would have understood. But her name would not be displayed in large red letters throughout shopping malls. She would not have been guesting on TV talk shows. Her cookies might have been famous, but only to her family and friends.

Another story worth mentioning is the one involving Mr. and Mrs. Silverman and Brad, their teenage son who was born with Down's syndrome. He has physical and mental handicaps, but through his courage and with the help and determination of his parents he has defied the odds. He has graduated from high school and will be entering college shortly.

When Brad was born, his parents were told of their son's probable limitations and what they could expect regarding his development. They could easily have given up, resigned themselves to the fact that Brad would not advance like other children in school and at home. People would have understood. But instead they decided to put all their love and effort into raising their son in as normal an environment as possible. They presented Brad with opportunities, and he excelled beyond their hopes or expectations. Brad's story was recently the subject of a TV Afternoon Special program. It emphasized the great courage and determination that Brad and his parents showed despite the obstacles they faced.

You may not readily identify with the Silvermans or with Mrs. Fields. Perhaps you are troubled by more immediate problems, such as the failure to learn something new in school, or a party you hosted that did not turn out well. Those frustrations are just as real and just as important to you.

You may be deeply hurt or angry at yourself for failing to notice someone's accomplishment. You may have failed to remember a close friend's birthday. Everyday we experience success and failtures. It may be just the inability to open a stuck door, or rushing to pick up your clothes at the cleaners only to find the store closed. What can be done to cope with these failure experiences? Let's find out.

Nobody Is Perfect

When something goes wrong, a number of emotions come to the surface. You may become immediately defensive, you may attack (verbally or physically), you may cry, or you may withdraw in silence. Everyone reacts differently in any given situation. It is important to realize that these types of reactions and feelings are common. Nobody is perfect. Try to forget your expectation of an ideal reaction to a situation. Don't be consumed with thoughts of, "If I were smarter or stronger I wouldn't have failed," or, "If I were better looking they would have chosen me." Develop the courage to be *imperfect* and accept a failure without undermining your own self-confidence. It is human to fall short, just as it is human to want to succeed, to want to live up to your ideals.

A handsome, popular movie star recently announced his wedding plans, much to the dismay of his adoring female fans. But in an interview shortly after the ceremony surprising comments were made about the star's wife. The fans told a reporter that they were no longer upset with their idol. They were, in fact, delighted with his choice of a wife. Why? asked the reporter. The fans explained that those who attended the ceremony noticed that the wife was nervous. Her hands shook and her voice trembled. She was on the thin side, had wild, unruly hair, and a mascara smudge on her cheek. They had expected *perfect*. She wasn't perfect; she was a "regular person". . . "like one of us."

> "When I fail at something I feel out of control. I feel as if other people are criticizing me and no one really cares how I feel. Why should anyone care or like me when I am a failure? I get upset and the whole world looks hopeless."
>
> Leah, 15

Learning to Voice Your Feelings

One of the most important things to remember when you do fail at something is to be easy on yourself. Let your emotions surface instead of keeping them bottled up inside. If you feel sad, cry. If you feel tired, rest. If you feel angry, yell. One sophomore told me that he has his own therapy for expressing his anger. He screams into his pillow at night with his stereo blasting rock music in the backround. He yells out all of his frustrations until his face turns red and he begins developing a splitting headache. Then he knows it is over and he can relax.

To deny your feelings is to keep yourself stuck in an emotional state of depression. Allow your feelings to surface and to be expressed. There are many ways to express feelings. Sonya chose to write her thoughts in her journals. Another girl goes for long walks by herself, in pouring rain, freezing cold, or scorching hot weather. She walks and she walks, pondering her problems and her choices. She talks to herself. When she finally reaches home she is in a better frame of mind. She has a clearer view of her feelings and what she plans to do.

Below are examples of *coping activities* that may help you overcome feelings of anger, depression, or despair after experiencing failure.

- Joining an aerobics class
- Horseback riding
- Bowling
- Painting
- Going to a concert
- Seeing a movie
- Going shopping
- Visiting a friend or relative
- Playing the piano
- Writing in a diary

When you choose to withdraw for long periods of time, clamming up and retreating to your room, you have too much time to think. You begin to dwell on how miserable you feel, and it becomes difficult to break out of the cycle. Sometimes just getting out into the fresh air can help. A simple walk to the corner mailbox may clear your head. Try to realize that each painful loss you experience becomes just another opportunity to shut down. And we know that it is far easier to shut down than to forge ahead toward another goal.

When people experience a devastating loss, such as the death or separation of a loved one, they are often steered by their doctor to a support group of people who have had like experiences. They are struggling with similar feelings of anger, loneliness, fear, but just being able to talk about it helps. By expressing your fears to someone else who knows, or who has been there, you are releasing the loss within yourself. You have brought it out into the open, and no one is laughing or criticizing you. They empathize with your feelings, and that in itself is a relief.

The same is true for young people. It may not be possible for you to attend a support group or to engage in a therapy session, but merely talking out your feelings with friends or family helps. Let go of your loss. Surely you will remember it and draw on it for years to come, but there is no use hanging on. It will be more harmful if you do. Use the lesson or experience to your advantage, then let it go—don't let it run your life.

Try the following exercise. Imagine for a moment that you hold your painful losing experience in the palm of your hand. Whether it be the frustration of not making

Student Council this year, or the fact that you betrayed a friend by failing to keep a secret, realize that you have two choices: You can take the loss and toss it to the wind, or you can close your hand and keep it close to you, thinking about it, nurturing it, feeling it, carrying it with you wherever you go. Now, if it's gone, you have nothing left but the memory, which will diminish in time. But if you hang on to it, it becomes harder, stronger, difficult to shake loose. It becomes an obstacle in your way, and you may have difficulty in seeing around it. It will always be there with you, blocking your way for change and new opportunity.

It's true, you may remember the fact that you betrayed a friend for many years to come, but you will also have learned something from that experience. You remember how upset and guilty you felt after you let the secret out. You may think twice about doing it again in the future. Let the loss work for you by using the experience to your advantage. Learn from it, then be willing to let it go.

Say Goodbye to Guilt

So many of us feel guilty when we fail at something. If a child ends up in trouble with the law, it's the parents who feel guilty. They feel that somehow they have failed as parents, even though they have other children who are well adjusted. Sometimes the guilt in parents is so strong that their own self-esteem rises and falls with their child's successes or failures.

How many of you feel guilty when something goes wrong in your life? Do you feel guilty when you try but fail to reach a goal? When you think about it, feeling guilty is a waste of time, because along with feeling guilty come feelings of worry and doubt—worry about not having done enough, or not saying the right things. Whether we realize it or not, the reason for feeling guilty often has nothing to do with the accomplishments or the failures themselves. Guilt may be a way of trying to communicate something to someone else. The *real* purpose of the guilt feeling may be:

- *To get sympathy*: "Poor you...we understand... maybe you'll make it next time."
- *To prove your worth*: I should not have won the prize...someone else may have needed it more than I.
- *To show how much you are suffering*: Look at me...I can't make it in this world...everything bad comes my way.
- *To control people:* If you take a job out of town, my health will fail and you won't be around to help me.

People who feel good about themselves don't have to bother with feeling guilty. They accept what is dealt to them, good or bad. If it is bad, they look for ways to make it good. Next time you find yourself feeling guilty about winning or losing, ask yourself, What is the real purpose of these feelings? Can I rid myself of this guilt and replace it with acceptance and change? At times all of us feel that we have not lived up to our standards, whether they be religious, moral, or standards of achievement. But that does not mean that a guilt feeling must follow. The dialogue below is an illustration of looking into guilt feelings.

Steve: I feel terrible. I feel so guilty that I wasn't accepted to Washington State.

Mr. Jones: Why do you feel guilty?

Steve: Because my parents had their hopes set on that university. Now I'll have to apply to another school. I feel that I really let them down.

Mr. Jones: Have they said that they are disappointed?

Steve: No.

Mr. Jones: Are they depressed, angry?

Steve: No.

Mr. Jones: Are you disappointed that you weren't accepted to Washington State?

Steve: Actually, I'm relieved. I didn't want to attend school out of state.

Mr. Jones: Then nothing really terrible has come out of this application rejection?

Steve: No.

Mr. Jones: So what kind of failure are we talking about...failure as a son? Or failure to make a university list?

Steve: Failure to make a list, I guess.

Mr. Jones: And guilty—

Steve: For having failed them—

Mr. Jones: Which you really didn't.

Steve: No, I did not.

Mr. Jones: There will be other lists—

Steve: And other opportunities.

"When I was fifteen I had to face the fact that my mother and father were getting a divorce. I couldn't do anything about it. I couldn't help but feel that I had failed them somehow. It made me feel lonely and depressed. Finally, I had a long talk with each of them and explained my fears and my feelings. They each told me that I had nothing to do with the breakup, that they loved me just as much, even more now that they would be living apart. I had to accept the fact that they did not want to live together, but knowing how they felt about me assured me that I hadn't failed as a daughter."

Joni, 17

Fear Not

Along with guilt and worry, many young adults carry with them various fears. They may fear:

- Not being liked.
- Not being in control.
- Not being sexually attractive.
- Becoming pregnant.
- Being critized.
- Being labeled a failure.

Let's use Jonathan's experience to illustrate the fear of being labeled a failure.

Jonathan is twenty-two. Over the years he had experienced general feelings of depression and anxiety. He had his first anxiety attack at the age of eighteen. Jonathan was shopping at a record store in a neighborhood mall. His symptoms came on suddenly: fast pulse, dizziness, sweaty palms, and a feeling that he was going to pass out. He was frightened and ran out of the store and back to his home. He was very much upset.

Although he had only the one attack, Jonathan became
a recluse, retreating to the safety of his bedroom. His
fears soon snowballed. Before long he was afraid to enter
a bank, the post office, grocery stores, and restaurants.
He spent all his time watching TV in his room. He kept
going over his anxiety attack, analyzing the symptoms
and expecting them to happen again. He had developed
what psychologists call *agoraphobia*, fear of open
places. Jonanthan felt week and defenseless and saw
himself spending the rest of his life in his room. He felt
that people did not understand what he was going
through, that he was a failure as a human being.

But some months later a change began to occur.
Jonathan became angry. He was angry at himself for
giving in to irrational fears. Thinking it over, he realized
that it was not shopping centers and restaurants that he
was afraid of. He was afraid of having another anxiety
episode while in those places. He realized that if he did
not immediately face his fear, it would rule him for the
rest of his life. It would make him dependent at the
young age of nineteen, never able to lead a normal life
outside his home.

And so Jonathan decided to stand up to his fear. He
started by going back to the store where he had experienced the anxiety attack. He became anxious in the
store and, sure enough, began experiencing the same
frightening symptoms. But this time he did not run
away. He acknowledged the fact that he was sweating
and feeling light-headed. Taking a long deep relaxing
breath, he continued to walk around the store, trying to
take his mind off what was happening. He rode with the
symptoms and continued about his business. Within
minutes the symptoms began to subside. Soon the anx-

iety had left his body. Over the next few months Jonathan revisited the very places that he had avoided in the past. He did experience episodes of anxiety, but they were fewer and farther between. It did not happen overnight, but gradually Jonathan became an independent individual. He became involved in life again and no longer felt a failure. In fact, he was proud of the major obstacle that he had overcome. He was proud of himself and what he had accomplished.

As we know, it is frightening to face what we fear, to step out into the unknown. But when you move into unknown areas, you must be willing to trust yourself and others. Often you may have to balance your act before you step out; you may have to wait until you feel it is the right time. If you are still hurting from your last loss, give yourself time to heal before you begin moving forward again. But don't let fear of the unknown hold you back permanently. Try not to feel, "I might hurt others by making a wrong decision, so I will do nothing," or, "I'm afraid that another failure will ruin everything, so I'll stay where I am."

It takes great courage to unlearn patterns of weakness and fear. But the potential for change is always present. As in Jonathan's case, anything that has been learned can be unlearned.

If you find yourself standing up to your fears, or trying to change from a lesser position to one of greater magnitude, keep close track of the process of the change. Reward yourself for initiating the change. Try to focus on the positive and let the negative behavior fade away.

In their book *Spare the Couch—Self-change for Self-*

improvement, Donald Tasto and Eric Skjei write, "If you expect the worst from your surroundings, chances are good that your attitude will deteriorate, this will affect your mood and other behavior and sure enough, you will be miserable." The best defense against bringing yourself down like that is to teach yourself to focus on the pluses rather than on the minuses in a given situation.

Let's review again the coping procedures after experiencing a loss.

- Be totally honest with yourself.
- Acknowledge your feelings of disappointment or anger.
- Learn to voice those feelings.
- Use the information that you learned from your mistake.
- Step away from the situation. It will give you new insights.
- Give yourself time to heal.
- Let go of the loss.
- Be open to other options and new opportunities.
- Adopt new patterns of thinking.
- Don't be afraid to step into unknown areas.

Failures in Communication

Looking back for a moment after you have failed at something, you may wonder, Did anything I said or did bright about the negative outcome? Was I too shy in the interview? Did I seem uninterested? Was I pushy on the first date? Sometimes without realizing it we give off signs or signals to other people that result in negative feedback. This may be done innocently, through dress, posture, grooming, movement, or expression. Think about it. How do you present yourself when you meet people? What do you tell them about you? When you have experienced a failed relationship, perhaps you may have been throwing off negative vibes. These could have been in remarks or in your attitude.

Do the following comments sound familiar to you?

- The movie was boring.
- The food was terrible.
- I'm so tired.
- I'm coming down with a cold.
- Do you think I'm attractive? Overdressed? Sexy? Smart?
- My feet hurt in these shoes.

These are not bad comments. We all tend to complain about things that bother us. But some people have a habit of saying all these things—whining and complaining—on a date. And then they wonder why the date failed, why they are not asked out again.

A poor attitude is enough to turn anyone off. Negative vibes can result in a negative relationship. Perhaps you need to reevaluate how you appear or how you sound to others. We give off positive and negative signals often without realizing it. When you are applying for a job or are meeting someone who will be making a decision about you, the signals you give off may make a difference in that decision. Below are some positive and negative signals.

Positive Signals	*Negative Signals*
A firm handshake	Nervousness
Maintaining eye contact	Avoiding eye contact
A genuine smile	Sighs of boredom
Eagerness to listen	Whining and complaining
Enthusiasm	Bragging
Good posture	Poor posture
Neat attire	Sloppy dress
Courtesy	Rudeness or sarcasm

Try looking at yourself through other people's eyes. When you come into a room, what do you think a first impression of you will be? Ask yourself: Would I like to have me as a member of the team? Would I like to have me as an employee? No matter how confident or sure of yourself you try to appear, you still project on the outside how you feel about yourself on the inside.

You may be inwardly excited that you are in the running for a school event, but your actions may show otherwise. The person who is lively, enthusiastic, and smiles genuinely gives off *positive signals*. The one who talks in a monotone, avoids eye contact, and maintains a sour expression may lose out to the former, even though both may be equally qualified to win. Here are some tips that may make the difference next time you are being considered for something important:

- Don't brag.
- Remember to say "Thank You" when you are paid a compliment.
- Greet people with a smile, extend your hand first, look that person in the eyes when you speak.
- Don't complain about your health, your aches and pains, or the weather.

- Don't put yourself down, saying, "I can't imagine myself being chosen," or "I know I won't make it, I'm not as good as the rest."
- If you are being interviewed early in the morning, come prepared. Don't stay up late the night before and come in tired and bleary-eyed.
- Don't chew gum or smoke during an interview.
- Thank the person in charge for giving you the opportunity.
- If you lose out to someone else, congratulate the winner.

The Winning Edge

It was narrowed down to two: Sam and Charlie. They were the finalists in the competition to represent the school as a foreign exchange student in Paris, France. Each boy was called in separately and interviewed by the committee. Charlie was the sure bet to win. He was an A student, had traveled throughout Europe, and spoke French fluently. In the interview, however, he came across as arrogant and uninterested. He bragged about his past experience with European girls. He chewed gum noisily and kept looking at the clock, anxious for the interview to be over.

When given the opportunity to ask questions, Charlie shrugged his shoulders and said he knew all he needed to know about the program. He said he was the best qualified in the school and wanted to be chosen.

Sam, on the other hand, was an average student. He spoke little French and had never traveled outside his hometown area. But he was excited about the possible opportunity to live abroad with another family, and it showed. He came prepared with a list of questions. He was enthusiastic and told the committee how much it would mean to him if he were chosen.

The committee came back with their decision the following day. While they admired Charlie's grade average and ability to speak French, they chose Sam. They were pleased with his eagerness and his honesty. They felt that he would be more appreciative of the chance to live with a family in another country. Sam made a better presentation, and because of that—he won.

As we have seen, failing at something, however big or small, can feel like the end of the world. But it can also be used as an advantage. Next time you experience a failure in your personal life, feel the loss for the moment. Express your feelings and remember them. Learn all you can from the situation. Ask yourself questions: Did I present myself well? Could I have done it differently? Then say goodbye and let it go. Remember that success involves learning, sharing, and growing. And that includes making mistakes along the way—mistakes that become our learning devices for getting closer to future goals and opportunities.

CHAPTER 6

Discovering Your Talents and Capabilities

The prospect of learning about ourselves can be frightening. While many of us expect to discover the worst, a hidden fear lies in the fact that we may also discover the best. If we fail at the same thing over and over again, we may need to stop and reevaluate what we are doing. It may be time to take a closer look at ourselves and what we really are trying to accomplish. We must ask questions such as, If this path is closed again, as it appears to be, where do I go from here? What else would I be happy doing? Feelings of self-doubt may begin to flood our minds.

- If I drop Marilyn, I may never have another girlfriend.
- If I don't score high enough on this English final,

maybe I should forget about a career in journalism.

- If I'm not accepted to this college, what use is it to
  try for others?

Discovering that we may not be able to achieve one
particular goal makes us anxious because it opens up the
possibility for change. And it is during this time of possible change that we begin to see ourselves in a new
light. How often have you found yourself accomplishing
something that surprises you. You say, "I can't believe
it, I didn't think I could do it, but I did." Or "I thought it
was the end of the world, but it turned out to be the best
thing that ever happened to me." You may discover
quite by accident in changing your course of action that
you have a talent for something different, such as singing
or acting or working with young children. Many times
our talents are not recognized until something happens
by accident that reveals them.

Stumbling upon a talent can be exciting. First you
may ask yourself, "Okay, I have it, but what do I do with
it?"

"I was an extra in an Off-Broadway stage production. At the last minute I was asked to stand in for
the lead, who had become ill. I fell right into the
part and it was fabulous. I sang and danced and
received a standing ovation and a number of curtain
calls.

Never in my wildest dreams did I think I could
elicit cheers from a crowd of admirers. The thought
of pursuing a musical stage career scares me, but I

now know I have the talent. I plan to do something about it.

Lilian, 19

Pursuing a dream may be one of the most difficult tasks that you'll ever have to do. Obstacles and disappointments will occur along the way, and not everyone can handle disappointment and forge on. Think for a moment about people that you know or know of who have overcome obstacles. You know of disabled people who have surmounted their disabilities, such as the armless artist who paints with her toes. Deaf people speak with their hands, blind people get around the city streets by themselves, using their sense of smell. These are admirable accomplishments. So was the election of President Jimmy Carter, former Georgia peanut farmer. A coal miner's daughter, Loretta Lynn, rose to the top as a country western singer. An overweight housewife, Jean Neiditch, devised her own diet and shared it with the world in Weight Watchers.

It can happen to anyone. It can happen to you. Think of something exciting that you would like to accomplish. Forget about the obstacles that would prevent you from reaching that goal: lack of money, inexperience, no connections. Just concentrate on a long- or short-term goal that you have always held.

- Become a rock and roll singer?
- Play the drums?
- Skate professionally?
- Become popular in school?
- Speak in front of a large group?

- Compete in the Olympics?
- Teach children?
- Work as an artist?
- Travel to another country?
- Run your own business?
- Lose weight?

Now close your eyes and imagine yourself having reached your goal. How does it feel? Can you see yourself in the part? Get in touch with what you would be doing, what you would be saying, how others would be reacting to you. Do you feel a sense of excitement or anticipation visualizing yourself doing what you really want to do?

Perhaps you have always dreamed of becoming a famous musician, a rock and roll star. You see yourself on stage, playing a guitar like no other. Your group is a household name, the fans adore you. The money is rolling in faster than you can count it. The music and fame are in your blood. You think, This couldn't be happening to me, it only happens to the Bruce Springsteens, to the David Bowies, to the Bryan Adamses.

Think again. Springsteen was not born with a hit song. He came up through the ranks of hopefuls like everyone else. You've heard the saying, "He paid his dues." Where, you may ask, does a dream like this begin? It begins simply with talent and a desire to run with that talent. It begins with music lessons and practice. It involves dealing with setbacks, turning your cheek to rejection, moving around obstacles and forging ahead.

Think of the person you most admire, someone who in your mind has made it. A teacher? A newsworthy person? An aunt who runs her own business? Your mother? Think of someone whose shoes you would one day like to be in. How do you suppose those people got where they are today? They had dreams and hopes just as you do. And they acted on them. The Streisands, the Redfords, the Rod Stewarts, your aunt, your mother, all were young adults once. They attended school and dealt with the same worries and frustrations that you deal with day to day. The ones you now admire were once in your shoes admiring someone else. They were *you* once, and you, if you set your mind to it, can become like *them*.

You can't get there, however, by simply wishing. Tossing your lucky penny into the fountain, or believing in your fortune cookie's promise will not do it; you're only kidding yourself if you think so. Because while you are wishing on your star, carrying around your lucky coin, and crossing your fingers, someone else has already put your plan into action. The *doers*, the *planners*, the *opportunity chasers* are passing you on the sidelines, waving at you as they race toward the finish line.

Perhaps you are thinking, I'd give anything to be a professional figure skater someday. Skating is so easy for me, I enjoy it and get a fantastic feeling dancing on ice. But. . .

- I'm not sure if I have the style or the grace to make it.
- I've heard it takes years of practice. My schedule is so full already.
- I get nervous just thinking about performing in front of an audience.

It's natural to want something but to question your ability. It's also easy to come up with excuse after excuse for *not* pursuing your dream. The hard part is pushing everything else aside and making the dream happen. Get ready to *shift gears* and to start thinking in a positive way. Turn "I'm not sure" into "I know I can." Prepare yourself for nervous times, for spills on the ice. Most skaters say that they experience jitters and worries about falling.

You can do it if you believe strongly in yourself and your ability to pull it off. Do you want to skate like the pros? Develop the style and the grace by watching others who are more experienced. Observe the way they move, their manner of dress, how they act. And be prepared to practice, even if it means rearranging your schedule to fit in lessons. Nervous about performing in front of an audience? Start small. Practice skating in front of a friend. Gradually begin to skate in front of members of your family, then a small group of people. Work up to performing in front of a crowd. It may not happen overnight, but with hard work and a *desire* to make it, you'll be ahead of those who are merely wishing and hoping.

Michael's Story

Not long ago, Michael sat down and wrote a Movie of the Week TV script. He had picked up a "How To" book at a bookstore so that he could type it in proper teleplay form. He had no experience, no agent, and no connections in the movie business. But he had a dream. "I wanted more than anything to see my story produced on TV," he explained. "I envisioned my family and friends sitting around the set with me one evening, congratulating me after seeing my name roll by in the credits."

As Michael was putting the finishing touches on his

script, he was told, "It's a long shot, don't get your hopes up." "You don't have an agent, they could steal your story." "Realize that you are a small fish in a big sea. There are a swarm of hopeful screenwriters out there submitting material."

He listened to the advice, but at the same time he wrote to a production company asking if he could send his story to them for a reading. They responded, and the script was mailed off to them along with a legal release form. "What happened next was amazing," Michael said. "Within a week I received a call from a producer at the studio. They liked my story and wanted to buy it. They wanted to know if I would talk terms or if I had someone who could represent me on the deal. This couldn't be happening so fast, I thought. I had no connections...I was a small fish in a big sea. But it was happening, and I was on cloud nine. I was already visualizing my new mansion in Beverly Hills."

Michael was on a high for seven days. Then, as so often happens in Hollywood, the deal fell through. They called to tell him that they were sorry, because they "absolutely loved the script"; however, they had decided to pass on the project and head in a different direction. Michael was devastated. He could not speak to anyone for the rest of the day. When his script was returned in the mail, Michael tossed it aside and vowed that he would never write again. However...

A few days later Michael received another call from the producer. They had been impressed with his script and liked his style of writing. The production company was in the talking stage of a new project and thought he would be perfect for an inside writing job. Was he interested? Michael was up again, on cloud nine. He was on a roller coaster of acceptance and rejection, but he began to realize some important facts about himself and his abilities. As Michael explained it, "I felt that I was right all along in believing that I had what it takes. I guess I should consider myself lucky, but I know I have the talent to write and I plan to pursue it. When people tell me the percentages against my making it, I will put myself in the opposing percentages for succeeding. I know I must expect a lot of rejections if I go into this field, but I will not let that stop me. I will accept the rejections that come my way and keep plugging away at my goal. Having stumbled upon my talent for writing dialogue and stories, I'm going to run with it and not look back."

Reaching for Goals

Take into account your abilities and also your weaknesses for doing certain things. What turns you on? People? Music? Applause? Friendship? What seems impossible for you to accomplish? Try to keep a realistic balance between the two as you develop your goals. Work at strengthening your weaknesses. The reason so many people fail to achieve their goals in life is that they give in to their weaknesses. They quit before they've even had a chance. And some never even get started. They talk about goals but never set them in the first place. They watch others with envy, thinking, Gee, I could have done that, or, I'm better than that person, why didn't I go for it? These people feel that they are not good enough in certain areas. They let their doubts and their weaknesses rule.

The following steps can take you from mere dream to

an accomplished goal. Try to fit your own situation into these steps. Make it happen for you too.

- Visualize yourself in a position that you have always dreamed about, something that you have always considered out of reach. Do you feel a sense of excitement? A sense of pride knowing that you are doing what you want to do?
- Ask yourself, What is really stopping me from reaching this goal? Is it more schooling? Money? Knowing the right people? Are these permanent obstacles, or can they be overcome?
- Devise a plan. Set short-term goals first. If you have a longing to be a fashion model but need to slim down, start now. Don't wait until the week before an interview.
- Don't run at the first sign that something may go wrong. Expect to meet setbacks, to experience some failure along the way. Include this in your plan so that you will not be thrown off course when a setback comes your way.
- Get your feet wet by doing volunteer work or by helping someone out without expecting to be compensated. You will gain valuable experience by watching someone else, by assisting, and by asking questions. Baby-sit to gain experience working with children. Run errands for a company you might be interested in working for in the future. Absorb what information you can that will help you arrive at your goal.

Realize that you can't set a goal to become a Kenny Rogers, but you can work toward becoming a successful country singer and songwriter. You can't become a Mrs. Fields, but you can become well known for your own delicious chocolate chip cookie recipe. It will take planning and action. Accomplishments do not materialize overnight. We don't become doctors in six months, scientists in three weeks. Great accomplishments are made up of small, steady actions, and it is these that you learn to value and work at. When taking small steps, you may not feel as though you have done a lot. But each step counts toward a finished project. Directed action, no matter how small, moves toward its point.

Learn to Challenge

When *they* say . . .	*You* say . . .
It can't be done.	Why not?
It's too risky.	Show me another way to get it done.
No one has ever tried it.	Let me be the first.
They are very professional.	I'm as good as the rest.
It's very difficult.	I'm willing to learn.

"To succeed in any form, challenges and risks must be taken. Whether they be great or small, they must be taken, because choices must be made in our lives daily. I tell myself not to get worried or elated over things that must be done; I accept this as part of life. When it comes to a challenge, I do it with courage and intelligently."

Sally, 18

"I don't mind a challenge. If you don't set goals, you will never find out if you can do something. You will always wonder about it. People learn from their mistakes, and every mistake you make is a risk you have dared to take. It's something to be proud of."

Tracy, 17

"I'm not one to take a risk going after something because of the possibilities. If I fail I have a hard time dealing with it, and it sets me way back. It's a long time before I will put myself out there again. I feel that most of the time when a person goes for a challenge, something goes wrong or something bad happens before the good comes about. I have to see the facts and know the outcome...it has to be written in black and white."

Kyle, 19

The following chart shows goals set by several students, their worries, and how they achieve their goals by using new plans of action.

Goal	Worries	New Plan of Action
Jim's goal is to become a professional drummer.	That he will never be able to have his own set of drums. That he wil not be accepted into a band. That after years of practice he may not be considered good enough.	To continue taking drum lessons. To make plans to lease a set of drums with an option to buy them later. Not to let audition rejections get in the way of his goal.
Stephanie wants to leave home and have her own apartment next	That her parents do not think she is mature enough. That she does not	To start showing parents her responsibility and independence.

Goal	Worries	New Plan of Action
year when she turns eighteen.	have furniture to set up in a new place. That she may regret the move after living alone for a time.	To save money, scout yard sales for furniture. To start looking for apartments that lease on a month-to-month basis rather than by the year.
New in town, Jason wants to become known at school, to make friends, and to be included in activities.	That no one will talk to him. That he will spend weekends alone and not be invited to parties.	To introduce himself to a few people he would like to have as friends. To make the first move if they don't. To find out their interests and strike up a conversation about them after class or at lunch. To invite someone over, to make an effort to gain at least one friend.
Mark's goal is to stop running away from the school bully.	That he will be laughed at by classmates for challenging the bully. That the bully will come down even harder on him if he doesn't walk or run the other way as usual.	To confront the bully in private and explain his feelings of anger and frustration. To ignore future taunts by the bully instead of reacting. To take the complaint to the principal if the

Goal	Worries	New Plan of Action
		situation continues.
Evan wants to pass the History final that is to be given in six weeks.	That he will freeze when it is time to take the test. That if he fails his total grade average will be pulled down. That if he fails he will have to repeat the class next year.	To take detailed notes throughout the semester. To ask questions when a fact is not clear. To review his notes weeks before the exam. To get to bed early on the evening before the exam; to come to class alert and prepared.
Janet wants to be chosen as a camp counselor next summer.	That she won't be chosen because she does not have enough experience. That if she is chosen, she may not have enough time to spend with her friends. That she will have to give up the cooking class she signed up for.	To volunteer as a Counselor in Training, working with the kids and gaining experience this summer. To get to know as many people as possible and to show the staff that she would be able to do the real thing next summer. To make plans to see her friends on weekends and to take the cooking class in the fall.

Goal	Worries	New Plan of Action
Marv's goal is to lose twenty-five pounds by his seventeenth birthday in six months.	That he would start another diet and fail just as he had on so many others. That he would lose the weight but gain it right back after reaching his goal.	To visit his doctor first and have him or a nutritionist devise a safe diet to fit his needs. To expect some setbacks along the way, to reach plateaus, to gain a few pounds, but not to let that make him give the diet up. To learn to change his eating habits so that he will be able to maintain his desired weight.

Cheryl wanted desperately to become a good cook. She had visions of turning out delicious recipes for family and friends. But there was a small problem. Cheryl couldn't boil two eggs in water. Everything she attempted to make failed miserably. The over-baked rubbery cake for her boyfriend's birthday was the last straw. Cheryl was angry with herself and frustrated with her inability to cook. Thinking over her situation, she realized that she had two choices. She could walk away from the whole matter and resign herself to the fact that she would never turn out a decent meal. Or she could go back over her mistakes and see *why* she was failing. She started by examining her habits and admitting the following:

- Cheryl always seemed to be in a hurry to get things done. Even in the kitchen she was anxious, running around at top speed, putting things together. She often forgot certain ingredients called for in a recipe. She would get distracted by something else and leave what she was making in the oven, overcooking or burning it.
- Her friends had a habit of teasing her about being a terrible cook. She liked the attention and played along with them, often turning out terrible meals as a joke. Soon she began to believe herself that she was not meant to turn out anything successful in the kitchen. When something went wrong, she was not surprised and did not take the time to find out why.
- Her mother was an excellent cook, but Cheryl never went to her for advice or watched how she did things.

Cheryl wanted to reach her goal to become an excellent cook like her mother. But to do that, she had to change. She had to make a commitment to herself to slow down, to observe her mother's ways in the kitchen, to be more attentive when following a recipe, to experiment and not let setbacks or a few failed recipes slow her down. She was on her way toward achieving her goal.

Accepting Change

Learning to change is like learning to drive a car or bake a new dessert. At first you fumble through the motions. It is strange and awkward. Many of us still have that scared little kid inside.

For example, entering junior high school for the first time. Talk about changes! First, there is learning to operate a locker combination, and that's no laughing matter. If the locker fails to open, your books don't come out. How do you explain that to your teacher? Besides locker anxiety, you have to memorize a new schedule of classes and how to get to each one. How many of you have lain awake at night trying to remember where your classes are? Grade school was never this complicated.

But there is hope. After the first few weeks it all seems to fall into place. Opening your locker is no sweat— could you really have been that worried about such an easy task? And making it around the school to your classes? You can do it without a backward glance. Like any new learning process, it gets easier with time and practice. Nothing is more exciting than knowing that we have the skills and the power to change.

Realize that you have the right to act and to choose and to change even though everyone around you may be saying, "Don't do it," or, "Wait for a better time." Map out your own plan and put it into action. If you must, move away from people who are standing in your way, people who are not helping you succeed.

If long-term goals seem out of reach at the moment, start by carrying out small notches of success and reinforce them. Remember that *small steps add up*. Don't expect immediate results. Some people hesitate and move backward at the first sign of failing, convinced that they are in over their head. It is important to ride with these setbacks. *Don't give up*. And most of all, learn to rely on your own capacity for making judgments. If you want to become a dancer and your girlfriend laughs and raises her eyebrows in surprise—laugh with her. Then go ahead and pursue your dream of dancing. Be willing to go that extra mile for yourself.

CHAPTER 7

Tony

Q: Tony, you are thirty-nine years old, a successful businessman, well known in your community. You have a number of employees, a big home, a family of four kids. You seem to have it all. Hearing about you and listening to you, you seem so confident. What I'd like to know is how it was for you in your earlier years, when you were a child eight or ten years old? Were you a confident kid also?

A: No, I was not.

Q: Why not?

A: I had no confidence, and I had no support from my parents.

Q: In what way didn't they give you support?

A: I don't believe my parents gave me either the emotional support or the backing that they should have given me.

Q: Were you shy at school?

A: I never tried to do much at school because I was convinced that I was not able to complete anything successfully.

Q: What were some of the things your parents said to you to make you feel that way?

A: One statement I will always remember is something they told other people about me: "He's a nice boy, but don't expect him to amount to anything."

Q: That must have hurt. Did they realize that it bothered you when they said that to people?

A: It wasn't a question of hurt feelings. I just assumed that what they were saying was the truth. It never bothered me in that respect.

Q: Because of what your parents said or thought about your abilities, did it make you somewhat hesitant to come forward in class or to volunteer answers?

A: Not necessarily. I just didn't have the desire to go beyond what was necessary.

Q: Somewhere along the line things must have changed. You are very ambitious now and have a great desire to succeed. When do you think this change came about?

A: It isn't a question of when and where, it is a question of necessity. It was born of necessity. It got to a point where I had to provide for my family. A failure cannot provide for a family. I turned myself around and was not a failure.

Q: What was your parents' reaction to your new drive for success?

A: To give you an example of what I am talking about, when I started my present business, which by the way has been successful for the past ten years, my parents' comment was, "Don't bother to take the risk; it won't make it; you won't succeed." At that point I wasn't thinking of whether I was going to fail; I was thinking of how successful I was going to be. I was finally convinced of my own ability to complete a task. I saw then that my parents were unable to perceive exactly who I was and what I was doing.

Q: Going back to your teenage years, was that a happy time for you?

A: As I look back on it, I perceived it to be an unhappy time, but the more I advance in age, the more I realize that the perceptions I had of myself were in error.

Q: Why did you perceive it as an unhappy time?

A: I never could have a good time. I made an attempt at suicide when I was in high school. I felt a general great need not to go on.

Q: Why did you attempt to commit suicide? What was pressing you or so difficult during that time?

A: Nothing that I could really put my finger on, other than that I was extremely unhappy. I was not successful at anything, I was not happy with what I was doing, who I was doing it with, with life in general. I felt that I didn't have control over my life. It made me extremely depressed. When I attempted suicide, I went through the motions but did not carry it through. I only made myself very sick, enough to put me in the hospital.

Q: Do you feel this was a cry for attention from your parents, to get them to notice your unhappiness and to be able to bring everything out in the open?

A: No, I don't think it was at all directed toward my parents. It was merely a cry for help, saying, "Look at me, I'm a person—I am not *nothing!*"

Q: Were you pretty much a loner during that time, or did you have friends?

A: I could count my friends on the first two fingers of my right hand.

Q: Today, as an adult, are you pretty much a loner?

A: Absolutely.

Q: Are you happy with it this way?

A: Now?

Q: Yes.

A: I would prefer to have more friends. On the other hand, I know I'm not easy to get along with.

Q: Back in high school, did you ever come up with any bursts of creativity, any exciting ideas that you wanted to pursue but did not, for fear of what your parents or others would say or think?

A: What my parents said or did not say never held me back. The only way it might have held me back was in the sense that I myself was convinced that I was worthless. Until I reached the point where I believed

I could actually do something and do it well, I was convinced that mediocrity was a way of life.

Q: Are your parents alive today?

A: No.

Q: If your parents could see you as you are today, a successful, confident, happy man, what do you think they would say to you?

A: They would probably come forth with the negative. Even if they could see me thriving in my business and personal life, they would probably find and emphasize any negatives—such as immaturity, my spending habits, questions as to whether I really am a good husband and a good father.

Q: So even though you are confident in your own mind that you have made it, you think they would still perceive you the same way—

A: Oh, yeah. What it amounts to is that rather than sitting around thinking I could have changed them or made them believe that I was a good guy and deserved recognition, I have finally concluded that it really doesn't matter what they thought of me. I loved them for what they were—my mother and father.

Q: Today, with your own children, do you find yourself carrying with you some of your parents' values in the raising of your kids?

A: Absolutely.

Q: Do you ever find yourself quoting your parents or

trying to hold back your child's creativity by thinking that he is not able to do something?

A: Just the opposite. If one of my kids wants to pursue his or her creativity, such as art or music, I tend to promote it. I want them to have a broader perception of who I am and how I relate to them than I ever did with my own parents.

Q: In your business operations today, how do you feel about taking risks?

A: I generally avoid taking a risk.

Q: Is there fear behind that? If something should go wrong, you'd have to answer—or possibly what others might think if something backfired?

A: I'm satisfied right now with my position. I see no reason to take risks. I'm hesitant about change, though I realize that change is a positive thing.

Q: Are you always on the lookout for new opportunities?

A: Not really.

Q: So you are rather content and satisfied with your life as it is right now.

A: Absolutely.

Q: If you could take the knowledge that you have today as an adult and go back to the time you were an adolescent, what would you have done differently?

A: I think I would have enjoyed the "moments" more, rather than always concentrating on the negative aspects. I would try to impress people more by performing adequately than by being outrageous.

Q: What advice might you give a young adult of today, who has high hopes and aspirations but has an obstacle of fear standing in the way?

A: Not to let fear be an obstacle, but to use it as a motivating element. If you fear a certain condition, seek out an alternative way to go on, so that you still have your options available. Failure is *not* the worst thing that could ever happen to you.

Q: Tony, thank you, and best of luck to you.

CHAPTER 8

Information Is Power!

S ydney Harrison is a marriage and family counselor, licensed by the State of Nevada. She has worked as a psychiatric social worker, counseling children and young adults at the University of Tennessee Mental Health Center in Memphis. Mrs. Harrison is a member of the Advisory Board of the Rainbow Child Care Center, as well as being a registered nurse. Currently, she is employed by the State of Nevada as an independent social worker, working with abused and emotionally troubled children. Sydney Harrison says:

"My very first piece of advice to teens is to have someone—a friend or counselor—to whom they can talk about wishes, ambitions, things that they would like to do but are afraid to try. Talk with that someone privately so you can express your feelings freely. Once you put your fears and insecurities into words with another person, it helps to lessen their power over your actions.

"When I talk to teens (and adults) I find out as much as I can about their wants. For example, if a girl wants to try out for cheerleader, I tell her to get specific information about what the auditioners are looking for. Do they want people who can dance and perform with music? Do they want aggressive gymnasts? Do they want a combination, or something very different? If she knows what they are looking for, she can tailor her audition to emphasize her own skills in that area. I had a sixteen-year-old recently who surprised her mother and everyone else by being chosen as a cheerleader, and she did so by following my advice. Joan and her mother both thought that she needed to know how to tumble, cartwheel, and form human pyramids, none of which Joan knew how to do. She and I agreed that she should go to the faculty adviser in charge of cheerleaders and ask how she should prepare for the tryouts. The adviser told her to work up a dance to any currently popular piece of music. Joan was able to demonstrate her coordination and enthusiasm (which, of course, the adviser was looking for) in ways in which she was well prepared and comfortable. Information helps eliminate the restricting anxiety associated with not knowing what to expect and gives us specifics to practice.

Rehearse and Practice

"Even if it's a young man making a phone call to a girl for a date, I find it extremely helpful for teens to rehearse. The new emphasis in sports psychology is on rehearsal—going over in one's mind in as much detail as possible all the specific details of a desired behavior. Swimmers, golfers, tennis players all benefit from mental practice, from explicitly visualizing what they want to do.

"I teach teens in my practice to do this. It's generally

pretty easy, since teens daydream or fantasize anyhow. I have them imagine the situation that they want, to picture clearly what it looks like in great detail, colors, shapes, who is wearing what. Then I have them say or do what they want and have them imagine themselves doing it well. Imagine how good it feels to do it well. Then I teach them *how* to do it well and have them rehearse it my way until they get that. Then we modify it to fit how they would do it.

"I often rehearse with them how to handle the unexpected or undesired so that in their fantasy they have covered all the possibilities and won't be caught unprepared. Again, I feel that it is important to be as *prepared* as possible in order to minimize the possibility of failing.

Learning Is Important

"If we do fail, however, then failure is an opportunity to learn, probably more than if we had succeeded. Of course that means that we have to instill in teens that *learning is important.* I believe it should be one of our highest criteria, and if I could say anything to every teen I would say '*Value learning.*' Life is a succession of opportunities to learn, and each time we are able to learn from experience we grow as a person and our life becomes richer and more fun.

"Being able to look at failure as an opportunity takes time to learn because we have first to deal with strong feelings. When we fail at something we can feel disappointment, sadness, anger. We can feel bad about ourselves and our abilities, or we can feel that we didn't prepare well enough, or we can feel rejected by other people. These strong feelings can be useful if we employ them as motivators in the right way. If we use them to decide, 'Oh boy, I don't want this to happen again'... and then figure out how to make sure it doesn't (without deciding never to take that particular type of risk again).

"I have a client, Mary, who is a beautiful, sweet seventeen-year-old and has never had a boyfriend. She has many boys as friends but is afraid to allow any of these friendships to develop into something more. When I asked Mary why she thought this was the case, she knew exactly why. She has seen many friends get hurt in relationships. She herself had been hurt in her relationship with her natural father and with her stepfather, both of whom were insensitive to women's needs. She had seen her mother hurt by these men. She loved and admired her mother but felt that because her mother made such poor choices in men, she was destined to do likewise.

"This obviously was a very limiting decision for Mary to make, especially since she made it as a result of mistakes and failures of others, not her own.

"What I did with Mary was to set her out to find examples of relationships that seem to be working and to learn as much as she could about how and why they work. She was not optimistic about the task but did succeed in finding two: One is a friend of hers, and one is her mother's friend. What she has learned so far is that there are decent, sensitive men in the world and that she can find one or several if she opens herself to seeing them.

"I do believe it takes a lot of effort to overcome the strong feelings associated with failure and to be able to move forward intellectually. You know, it's a difficult journey to go from gut feelings up to the brain and all the resources our thinking powers possess. Teens need encouragement and reassurance to know that each experience they have, whether or not it turns out well, goes into their own library of resources to be used later when needed.

Trying New Things

"My final piece of advice to teens is to try as many new things as possible. We never know for sure what we will enjoy or what hidden ability we have, and the more things we do that we enjoy and can do well, the more fun life is.

"I tried two new things myself this year, ocean kayaking and cross-country skiing. Both were activities I had never considered doing until a friendship developed with someone who loved doing them and wanted me to share in them.

"I am not athletic, and my image of myself does not include coordination nor physical strength. I took lessons in both sports and ended up as the star of each class, a fact that astonished and delighted me, since it was such a contradiction of my beliefs about myself. So now I have new information about my abilities and new, fun things to do. *Information* is power—the more we know about what we want to do, the greater is our chance of succeeding."

CHAPTER 9

What Really Matters

G etting in touch with our true selves is something we must do alone, by ourselves. We can't
look to others for advice on how we feel, think,
or act about relationships or events in our lives. When
we develop the confidence to look inward and accept
who we are, it becomes easier to relate outwardly to
others.

We all need time to quietly get to know ourselves and
to express our thoughts. This may mean breaking away
from the crowd and going off alone for a time to put our
thoughts in perspective. During this time we may learn
what is important to us, the things we like or don't like,
the things that excite us or that we find boring. Our
potential for creativity may come to life.

For many people, overcoming a failure experience can
seem like the end of the world. You do not know where
to run, what to do. You may panic and do nothing, afraid
of what might happen if you make a move. In this
situation you have to do something to get back on the

track. In some way, large or small, your life has changed. While it may be more comforting to retreat or to ignore what has happened, going forward—even into the unknown or unfamiliar—is a step in growth.

A mother with young children who has depended on her husband for everything may be in for a rude awakening if her husband divorces her or dies. She will be forced out into the world on her own. She will have to think for herself and make decisions. She will have to change because other lives are dependent on her. In Chapter 7, Tony talked about the necessity to put his past feelings of failure behind him in order to provide for his own family. You may one day find yourself pushed out of your secure nest, out in the world to think and to act on your own. There may be no one around to advise or help you. What do you do? Simple. You think and you act on your own. And gradually, over time, it becomes second nature, like finding your way around a new school. You may discover that your potential for success is far greater than you ever thought possible.

Those who are afraid a take a risk are often afraid of failing. What they don't realize is that successful people feel the same way. Many performers talk about being nervous when going before the cameras. The popular kid in your class is probably sweating it out before his turn to speak in front of the school assembly. You own teacher may have spent a few sleepless nights preparing to meet you on her first day of class. These people are nervous and jittery and frightened, but they *go*. They realize that it okay to be afraid. It is human.

Next time you have the opportunity to meet someone whom you admire, someone who you feel has made it, ask how he or she did it. Chances are, you will not hear a tale of instant success. What you will hear is the story of a person who has tackled many frustrations, many anxieties, and many setbacks.

Throughout these chapters we have talked about various methods used to cope with failure. We have heard from Sonya, from Karen, from Kirk, and many others about their thoughts and feelings on the subject. It is important to realize the scope of the feelings that we are dealing with. To one person, failure to pass a simple quiz may be more devastating than failing to be chosen for class office. Failing to make the football team may be a minor inconvenience to someone else, but failing to show up on time for tryouts in a play? The worst thing that could possibly happen! No two problems are alike. What is important to one may not be worth a passing thought to another. What *really* matters is your own situation, what is important to *you*.

When you fail at something that is important to you, a number of feelings and emotions come to the surface. Learning to admit these feelings and to accept them is a very important first step. Spinning your wheels from the sting of losing or of not making it will not get you very far. The pattern needs to be broken, and you can do it.

The major concern that has been stated over and over throughout this book by so many young people is *fear*, the fear of what others might say or think if they fail. Or how others might feel about their own personal choices. The mere thought of being laughed at or of being embarrassed in front of others is enough to stop some people in their tracks.

Learning to ride with criticism, learning to turn a deaf ear, to let others have their say but to go ahead with your plan, takes courage. And that is what much of this book has been about: courage. The courage to persist when the end seems so far out of reach; the courage to go straight for your goal despite obstacles in your way; the courage to learn from your mistakes. Now, at thirteen, sixteen, or nineteen, the future may seem a lifetime away, but it is closer than you think. We are here for such a very short time. And because of that, we must work at making the most of our lives, at giving and receiving, at sharing, at loving. Life is full of exciting challenges and opportunities, opportunities that do not discriminate against race, religion, or money.

As was discussed in Chapter 6, there are those who will sit back and *think* about going after opportunities and those who will actually go out and *pursue* them. Set the wheels in motion. Decide that you will be the one who *does* rather than *thinks* about it. Whether it be the desire to learn a new skill or just renew an old friendship, you are already two steps ahead if you have set your plan in motion.

Remember that your past, your present surroundings, or your financial ability all take a back seat to your *drive* and your *desire* to succeed. You have heard the expression, Where there's a will there's a way. Think about it. Use the information from this book to get started. Promise yourself that you will put your fears on the back burner and set about to change. Prepare to take the challenge. Forge ahead with new strengths, new determination, and never give up your dream.

Bibliography

Berne, Patricia H., and Savary, Louis. *Building Self-esteem in Children.* New York: Continuum Publishing Co., 1982.

Bolles, Richard Nelson, *The Three Boxes of Life and How to Get Out of Them.* Berkeley, Calif.: Ten Speed Press, 1978.

Crystal, John, and Bolles, Richard N. *Where Do I Go from Here with My Life?* New York: Seabury Press, 1984.

Dyer, Wayne. *The Sky's the Limit.* New York: Simon & Schuster, 1980.

Emery, Gary, Ph.D. *Own Your Own Life.* New York: New American Library, 1984.

Gould, Robert L., M.D. *Transformations.* New York: Seabury Press, 1984.

Oates, Bob. *The Winner's Edge.* New York: Mayflower Books, 1980.

Powell, Douglas H. *Teenagers: When to Worry and What to Do.* New York: Doubleday, 1986.

Waitley, Denis. *The Double Win.* New York: Berkley Books, 1985.

Weisinger, Hendrie, and Lobsenz, Norman M. *Nobody's Perfect.* Los Angeles: Strafford Press, 1981.

Index